SUPPORTING TEENAGERS THROUGH GRIEF & LOSS

SUPPORTING TEENAGERS THROUGH GRIEF & LOSS

Practical Ideas & Creative Approaches

Anna Jacobs

HINTON HOUSE Therapeutic Resources

Published by

Hinton House Publishers, an imprint of Loggerhead Publishing Ltd

Park Farm, Preston Deanery, Northampton, NN7 2DY

www.hintonpublishers.com

© 2013 Anna Jacobs

First published 2013
Reprinted 2016, 2024

All rights reserved. The whole of this work including texts and illustrations is protected by copyright. No part of it may be copied, altered, adapted or otherwise exploited in any way without express prior permission, except in accordance with the provisions of the Copyright, Designs and Patents Act 1988 or in order to photocopy or make duplicating masters of those pages so indicated, without alteration and including copyright notices, for the express purpose of instruction and examination. No parts of this work may otherwise be loaded, stored, manipulated, reproduced, or transmitted in any form or by any means, electronic or mechanical, including photocopying or storing it in any information, storage or retrieval system, without prior written permission from the publisher, on behalf of the copyright owner.

British Library Cataloguing in Publication Data
A CIP catalogue record for this book is available from the British Library.

ISBN 978 1 906531591

Printed and bound in the United Kingdom

Contents

List of Activities — vii

List of Worksheets — ix

About the Author — xi

Introduction — 1
    The Basics of Loss — 1
    How to Use this Book — 3

1 Adolescent Development and Theories of Bereavement & Loss — 7
    The Developmental Stages of Adolescence: a Transition — 7
    Attachment Theory — 8
    Theories of Grief — 9

2 The Grief Process in Adolescence and its Implications — 13
    Differences between the Adolescent and Adult Experience of Loss — 13
    The Stages of Grief — 17

3 How Adolescents Express Loss & How to Support Them — 21
    Physical Reactions to Loss (Mild) — 22
    Physical Reactions to Loss (Severe) — 24
    Emotional & Psychological Reactions to Loss (Mild) — 27
    Emotional & Psychological Reactions to Loss (Severe) — 39
    Sleep Issues & Spiritual Responses to Loss — 48

4 Questions & Comments from Adolescents   55

   On Death   56

   On Behaviours & Responses to Loss   62

   On Schoolwork & Friends   68

   On Social Media & Related Contacts   71

5 A Toolkit of Activities   77

   Guidelines for using the Activities   78

6 Resources   211

   A Sample School Bereavement Policy   212

   Template for a Letter to a Family Following Bereavement   214

   Template for a Time-Out Card   215

   Sample Group Contract for Adolescents   216

   Plan for a General Assembly on Bereavement   217

   Information on Anti-Bullying Policies   219

   Further Reading   221

   Useful Websites   223

   Music, Poetry & Art Resources   225

References & Bibliography   227

Activities

General Activities on Issues Related to Grief & Loss

1 The Loss Journal	84
2 The Space Story	93
3 Discussion about Bullying	96

Activities for Enabling Feelings

4 A Collage of Feelings	103
5 The Scale of Feelings	105
6 Music & Emotions	109
7 The Island	113

Activities for Working with Specific Feelings

Anger

8 Wild Animals Drama	118
9 Moulding My Anger	121
10 The Shape of My Anger	124
11 A Story of Loss	128

Sadness

12 Drawing My Sadness	132
13 Drama Exercise	135
14 Questions about Sadness	138

| 15 Poetry & Sadness | 142 |
| 16 A Story of Loss | 147 |

Fear & Anxiety

17 Causes of Fear	151
18 Drama Exercise	156
19 Reflections	159

Happiness

20 What Makes You Happy? (1)	168
21 What Makes You Happy? (2)	171
22 Music & Happiness	174

Insecurity & Withdrawal

| 23 Masks | 178 |
| 24 Clay & Poetry | 182 |

Memories

25 'I remember when …'	187
26 Memory Book	189
27 Art Activity	193
28 Memory Bowl	195

Relaxation

| 29 Relaxation Exercise | 99 |

On Death & Dying

| 30 How do You Feel about Death? | 202 |
| 31 Questions about a Bereavement | 204 |

Worksheets

1	The Loss Journal, Week 1: Introduction to Journal Writing	87
2	The Loss Journal, Week 2: Feelings	89
3	The Loss Journal, Week 3: Memories	90
4	The Loss Journal, Week 4: Things that Have Changed	91
5	The Loss Journal, Week 5: The Future	92
6	The Space Story	95
7	What do You Think of Bullying?	98
8	The Scale of Feelings	107
9	The Scale of Feelings: Discussion & Reflection	108
10	Music & Emotions	111
11	The Shape of My Anger	127
12	Excerpt from *Rory's Story* (1)	129
13	Questions about Sadness	139
14	Suggested Sad Poems	145
15	Excerpt from *Rory's Story* (2)	149
16	Fear	153
17	Anxiety in My Life	161
18	Dealing with Anxiety	165
19	Feeling Happy	169

20 What Makes You Happy?	172
21 Memory Book	191
22 My Experience of Loss	206

About the Author

Anna Jacobs is a qualified play therapist and creative arts therapist/counsellor, who is passionate about the needs of bereaved children and young people. She has been supporting bereaved children and their families for more than fifteen years, and has been a therapist and counsellor for more than twenty-five years. She has established and co-ordinated two pioneering Children & Young People's Services in the fields of cancer and palliative care in Lancashire and Cumbria and the South West of England.

Anna has supported children and families with many different types of loss, including serious illness, divorce and separation, sudden loss, extreme forms of bereavement such as murder and suicide, as well as those losses experienced within the care system. She has offered numerous trainings to social care, school and health staff and foster and adoptive carers on attachment theory, bereavement and loss. Her vision has always been that every child will have access to excellent local bereavement services and that every professional and family can understand the needs of children who have experienced loss.

She is the author of the popular resource, *Supporting Children through Bereavement & Loss* as well as *Rory's Story*, *Lucy's Story* and *Changes*, therapeutic stories with exercises to help teenagers, children and the very young to understand the experience of loss and bereavement. She is the co-author, with Lorna Miles, of *Supporting Fostered & Adopted Children through Grief & Loss*.

Introduction

> And death shall have no dominion.
> No more may gulls cry at their ears
> Or waves break loud on the seashores;
> Where blew a flower may a flower no more
> Lift its head to the blows of the rain; ...
> And death shall have no dominion.
> (Dylan Thomas, 'And Death Shall Have No Dominion',
> *Twenty-five Poems*, 1936)

The Basics of Loss

One thing is certain in our lives – eventually we will die. Another thing that is equally certain is that at some point we will experience the death of someone close to us. The experience of losing a person to death is called loss; but loss can also come from other causes, such as separation, divorce and emigration. This book will primarily explore the needs of adolescents when they experience loss from death, as well as from other causes.

Generally, in society, we expect that young people will experience loss infrequently. That is to say, we do not normally expect young people to have a deeper experience of loss in their early lives and hope that they may be able to reach adulthood with little major loss in their lives. However, more and more adolescents are experiencing what may be termed major loss at a younger age. Many may experience the death of a pet or the loss of a grandparent (who may or may not have been close to them), or they may even experience a house move as a loss. However, the loss of a parent, parental figure or sibling from death, separation or divorce is on the increase, as are losses from such things as suicide and accidents.

Research published by Shipman *et al* in 2001 found that 79 per cent of all schools had children on their roll who had been bereaved of a close family member within the previous two years. Harrison and Harrington (2001) estimated that by the age of sixteen 6 per cent of young people would have experienced the death of a parent. In addition, Silverman and Worden (1992) found that two years after a parental death self-esteem was significantly lower among bereaved young people. These are not insubstantial figures, and show that a significant number of children and young people do experience a more profound loss and are potentially affected by it.

Introduction

In the past, for instance in Victorian times, when death and loss were a more everyday part of life, young people of all ages took part in mourning rituals alongside their parents and relatives, and the body was normally viewed by all before being buried. Children grew up very quickly, and were expected to work from a young age, even as young as 8 years old, so it was logical that they were more involved in the rituals of life and death. Other non-Western cultures do have more open rituals for burial and loss, such as Indian cultures that burn their deceased openly and mourn in the streets.

In recent times, certainly in the West, young people have not regularly been included in funeral rituals, even of their parents. Indeed, from approximately the beginning of the twentieth century, parents began to regard young people's attendance at funerals, and even their acknowledgement of death, as inappropriate and irrelevant. We in the West in particular appear to have divorced ourselves from the process of death and dying. Funerals and funeral directors take over the process, and religious ministers are the ones who minister, even to many who no longer have any faith or to those whose faith differs from their own. Many adults today will remember a lack of involvement as young people, when a family death was not mentioned; they were not expected to attend any mourning or ritual and were not included in the details. They often have only a hazy recollection of a father or mother (or significant other relative, such as sibling) disappearing, without any real explanation. They may not have discovered all the details of what happened until many years later.

There could be said, however, to be a recent revival of interest in how to involve all family members, including young people, in the rituals of death and dying. Alongside this is a growing interest in both the communication of matters connected to death and bereavement, and how the processes of family mourning and funerals take place. Organisations such as the Dying Matters initiative; and Childhood Bereavement Network and Child Bereavement UK (see Resources, 'Further Reading') are a significant part of enabling some of these changes. It is the hope of all these organisations, and of the author, that the current situation, in which many families and professionals have difficulty in both speaking about and involving young people in the processes and rituals connected to loss, can move to one of more openness and confidence.

Professionals and parents/carers who are in regular contact with young people are often confused about what to say, and how to support young people when death and loss occurs. Yet with a few guidelines, clear suggestions, and understanding of what is most helpful, they could be less fearful and more influential in supporting such young people. Adolescents experience loss and grief in a very similar way to adults, yet many adults are hesitant when approaching such young people. Their need is to have opportunities to talk about and explore their feelings and reactions to loss. The experience of loss and grief is a very real and often shocking life lesson for this young people of this age, and can often lead to changes in life circumstance, character, future plans and perception of life.

There are many and various reasons why an adult may hesitate or lack confidence in supporting such young people. Sometimes it is simply lack of experience in using the language of loss, given the history already mentioned. Death and dying are still often taboo subjects, and there may be a fear of upsetting the very young people who need to speak and share their loss and feelings with someone. At other times it is because the act of speaking about the loss that a younger person has suffered may remind the adult of their own losses. In addition, in certain communities bereavement through unnatural causes may be so rare that when it does occur (in a school, for example) carers and other professionals are not fully prepared.

Loss itself is normal, however. When we love someone, we risk losing someone. Adults know this and live with this. Young people, however, are beginning to face this just at the time when they are beginning to face the loss of their own childhood. It is a time, therefore, of transition. Early loss happens in babyhood, when a mother walks out of the room and the baby cries deeply, feeling as if their world has ended. This is loss in its basic primeval form. As human beings we are bound to experience loss, just as we experience life, love, death, and the deeper feelings of fear and, hopefully, courage. Adolescent loss is intensified and complicated by the transitional nature of these years: childhood is coming to an end, adulthood is on the horizon, and the young person's awareness of the larger world is much stronger – but they are still in the midst of this change.

Due to the work of organisations such as the Childhood Bereavement Network, Child Bereavement UK and other excellent services within the UK, together with a growing body of theory on childhood bereavement, children and young people experiencing loss are now more able to access support. This book aims to add to the growing list of supportive literature in a clear, concise and reasonably simple way, so that those adults who still feel lacking in confidence about how to support a bereaved young adolescent, or one whose loss is from another cause, can begin to gain the necessary skills.

How to Use this Book

This book follows on from the first in the series, *Supporting Children through Grief & Loss* (Jacobs, 2013) which was concerned with how to support younger children through their experience of grief and loss. Both are inspired by the many professionals, including teachers, who have asked me questions such as: 'How do I speak to young people?'; 'What do I say?'; 'What do they need?'; 'Can I mention the word "death"', and so on. These questions were often asked at training sessions or, more significantly, when offering therapeutic support or advice and guidance for individual young people in their schools and health clinics. The teachers and others often felt a lack of confidence and hesitancy, which is common while attempting to support young people who are bereaved.

Introduction

Although this book has primarily been targeted at teachers and school assistants, it can also be used by health professionals, social services professionals, parents and others. It has a clear structure, beginning with some theories on bereavement and development, covering aspects of how to support adolescents and what to watch out for, followed by some creative activities and resources. The hope is that it will guide adults through the different aspects of loss when adolescents need support, and provide guidance on monitoring if they need extra support. It examines some questions teenagers may have, and gives suggestions as to how they may be answered. There is a chapter on what to watch out for, which includes some developmental factors for the older age range. There is a resources section at the end of the book, which includes websites and further reading.

Within the book there are some simple exercises to use with adolescents experiencing loss, with different categories of need. These include dealing with feelings, memories and telling the story, and issues related to death and dying. These are photocopiable resources that can be used as appropriate, and guidance is given on when and how to use them. Exercises are a very valuable method of supporting young people through the different aspects of loss and, by using them, professionals become confident in supporting the needs of bereaved teenagers or others experiencing loss.

The therapeutic tale of *Rory's Story* (Jacobs, 2014) may be used alongside this book in lessons and groups to enable young people to address their needs and discuss together the impact a bereavement or loss can have on them. It also has some guidance for teachers regarding different aspects of loss in adolescents and the use of the story.

This workbook does not need to be read through from cover to cover. It is a manual that offers simple, clear ways to understand and support grieving adolescents, and gives adults greater confidence in doing this. By the end of the book most adults should begin to feel confident enough to offer at least some support when a young person they know is suffering from bereavement or loss.

Chapter 1 discusses the theories behind supporting adolescents in grief and loss, and links these theories to the adolescent's own stage of development. This chapter gives some of the background to understanding the needs of such young people and indicates in various ways how supportive it can be, for example, to enable young people to mix with others or create a memory store.

Chapter 2 examines the grief process in adolescence and some implications for those supporting them. It particularly highlights the difference between the grief of an adult and a young person, together with some of the stages that might be experienced.

Chapter 3 describes how adolescents express loss, with some specific ways to support them, including examples of supportive comments in real situations, case studies to illustrate the possible scenarios a young person may present with, and comment on what has been experienced as helpful in differing circumstances.

Chapter 4 looks at questions, responses and comments in four areas that are particularly important to young people: death, behaviours and responses to loss, schoolwork and friends, and issues of social media. It anticipates some of the comments young people can make, and some questions they may raise when experiencing different forms of loss, and offers various suggestions of how to respond appropriately.

Chapter 5 is a large toolkit of activities, designed for various types of support at home, in the classroom and elsewhere. It includes group exercises, some exercises suitable for the many types of reaction to loss, and some classroom activities related to death and dying. It is user-friendly, with photocopiable worksheets and can be dipped into as needed.

The book ends with a chapter of resources and references. There are a variety of useful templates, such as a suggested school bereavement policy, a letter home to a bereaved family, a school 'time-out' card for a young bereaved person, and a suggested programme for an assembly on bereavement. There follow suggestions for books to use in various circumstances to do with loss and grief, useful websites, ideas on music and art for group work and a summary of current anti-bullying policy in the UK.

Chapter 1
Adolescent Development and Theories of Bereavement & Loss

> There are more things in heaven and earth, Horatio,
> Than are dreamt of in your philosophy.'
> (William Shakespeare, *Hamlet*,
> Act 1, scene V)

The study of bereavement and loss as experienced by young people has been expanding since the late 1990s in particular, and during that time there has been a growing body of research both on the theory of loss and the way in which children and young people can best be helped. Whereas the first book in this series, *Supporting Children through Grief and Loss* (Jacobs, 2013), covered bereavement theory and some related influential theories, this book refers to a wider body of research. The specific stage of adolescence holds its own challenges and needs, so including an overview of the developmental stage of adolescence is vital if we are to understand the needs of young people of this age range.

The Developmental Stages of Adolescence: a Transition

In order to place theories of grief within the context of adolescence, it is first important to understand the stage of development that adolescence represents, as well as its relationship to family and peers. Adolescents are going through a time of transition prior to reaching adulthood. Erikson, who developed a psychosocial theory for all stages of childhood and adulthood, spoke of this stage of development as that of 'Identity vs. role confusion' (Erikson, 1950), in which teenagers are beginning to create their own self-identity and role for their future as an adult. However, part of this transition is away from their exclusive loyalty to their family relationships and towards their loyalty to their peers and future partner. They are moving towards autonomy as individuals, while remaining dependant on their parents or carers and the wider family network until the later stages of adolescence. Erikson proposed that this stage functions mainly to develop a sense of self and identity, and that this ideally leads to fulfilment and competence. Failure to achieve this successfully therefore leads to a sense of inferiority, amongst other things.

As adolescents are developing and forging closer networks with their peers, while still remaining loyal to their parents, it follows that the loss of a parent or significant other carer could prove problematic or disruptive to this stage of development. The loss of a parent or carer from death, in particular, could be said to severely interrupt this developmental stage. Some researchers on adolescence have shown that at certain stages of adolescence, in particular the middle years of approximately ages 12 to 14 years, there is a lower level of self-esteem and resilience, and that there exists a level of vulnerability that could be exacerbated by a loss occurring at this stage. See, for example, Susan Hartner's study on self-esteem (conducted from 1987 to 1990), and Bee (1995) for a broader discussion of this. Bee commented on the findings of two studies (Achenbach & Edlebrock, 1981; Rutter *et al*, 1981), which showed that 40 per cent of teenagers were 'described by their parents or teachers as appearing miserable, unhappy, sad or depressed'. This is a high percentage overall, when compared to a figure of 10 per cent for the pre-adolescent stage.

These studies highlight the fact that adolescence is a time of vulnerability and change, which could be further exacerbated by an experience of grief and loss.

Physiological and emotional transition

Other factors clearly associated with adolescence are the physical, hormonal and emotional changes leading to the development of full sexuality. These changes influence an adolescent's exploration of their relationships, as young people are constantly experimenting with new ways of relating, with sexuality and often with changes in behaviour. These changes in hormone levels and physical appearance are accompanied by changes in mood and character, as adolescence develops further, leading to behaviours such as rebellion, withdrawal from family life and difficulties in communicating with parents and teachers. If an experience of severe loss occurs during this phase, there is an interruption of the process of transition from young adult to adult. This can be extremely disturbing for young people and cause complications in the process of forging a full identity and subsequently in forming successful relationships in adulthood. When supporting such young people, it is, therefore, vital to remember the vulnerability of teenagers.

Attachment Theory

Following on from these studies on the developmental stage of adolescence is a very influential theory related both to development and grief and loss – that of attachment. Originating with John Bowlby (1973), this theory refers to the bond that all human babies and children hope to make with their parents and carers, thereby forming a secure base from which children, growing up to be young people and adults, view and experience the world. There are a number of styles of attachment discussed within the theory: secure attachment (the ideal); ambivalent and avoidant insecure attachment; and the most severe of all, disorganised attachment. The styles of attachment formed in childhood have been found to have a direct influence both on adolescent behaviour and on the capacity to grieve and manage loss successfully, as well as affecting self-esteem, future relationships and emotional literacy. It is therefore a profoundly important theory with regard to how adolescents experience grief and loss, as adolescents are forming future relationships, examining their sense of self and developing resilience and self-esteem, and are already more at risk simply due to their stage of development.

Although this theory was first proposed in the late 1960s and 1970s, it is still being developed today. It has been found that those young people who have developed secure attachments to their parents and carers (that is to say, those who were successful, safe and secure in themselves at a younger age and show signs of resilience, the ability to show warmth and empathy, and develop appropriate relationships to their peers) are more successful in their ability to grieve appropriately, manage their feelings and successfully move beyond this to healthy adulthood (Dyregrov, 1991). Researchers such as Crittenden have developed the theory even further, examining the link between neuroscience and attachment theory, and devising an assessment process for both parents and young people that can indicate the style of attachment between both, and the way in which this may be used to influence mental health and other services (Crittenden, 2008; Crittenden & Landini, 2011).

Theories of Grief

Within the fields of bereavement and grief specifically, there are particular theories that have influenced those offering support to adolescents. Writers such as Elizabeth Kubler-Ross and William J. Worden are particularly significant. Kubler-Ross, well known for her seminal work, *On Death and Dying* (1969), proposed that grief involved the stages of denial, anger, bargaining, depression and finally acceptance. Although not now regarded as stages that are necessarily followed through in this sequence, those who have experienced loss or grief can certainly acknowledge that these are all stages experienced during a journey into and beyond grief. Although proposed in 1969, this theory is still relevant for people of all ages, particularly adolescents, who can often show anger, depression and bargaining very clearly in their responses to loss, including loss from causes other than bereavement.

William Worden expanded on Kubler-Ross's work and identified what he termed 'tasks for mourning' (Worden, 1996). These are:

1   accepting the reality of loss;
2   experiencing the pain of grief;
3   adjusting to an environment where the deceased is missing; and
4   reinvesting emotional energy.

These 'tasks' are also evident when observing and supporting adolescents who are facing a loss from another cause, such as separation or divorce. Such theories have influenced the services that now exist for young people who have been bereaved and can be used as a guide for those supporting adolescents. They also help by acknowledging that adolescents will, for example, become angry at one point, or show denial that the loss has happened, which is then reassuring for those carers and professionals who are offering ongoing support.

A newer growing body of work is in the field of neuroscience and how it relates to young people who experience trauma and loss (Perry & Hambrick, 2008). Research has shown that the parts of the brain that are affected by stress, the frontal lobes, become charged with chemicals that inhibit a person's ability to empathise or recognise their own emotions clearly. It shows that the brain responds chemically to triggers in our environment such as trauma and loss, and that emotion and empathy shown to a young person will enable a change in these chemical responses. The research has also revealed that growing, childhood brains are elastic and subject to change and that this growth does not stop until young adulthood. This body of knowledge, therefore, is influential both in helping us to understand the reactions of adolescents to grief and loss, and also in helping to shape current and future support services (Sunderland, 2007).

Another interesting field related to adolescent grief and loss is that of narrative theory. Grieving people of all ages are known to need to tell their stories of loss. Narrative theories propose that telling the story helps to make meaning of the loss and to create a new meaning based on shared stories with family and others (Neimeyer, 2001). The 'continuing bonds' theory is linked to the narrative approach, as it refers to the need for young people to refer to their past connections in order to move forward in their development, often finding narratives of their lives to assist them (Klass *et al*, 1996).

This theory states that young people continue to reframe memories of the person who is deceased, along with their feelings, which they then refer back to at key points in their lives in order to maintain the bond that was there before the loss. This enables a healthy continuation of their growth and development. Continuing bonds theory guides practitioners in the use of memory boxes and books in order to maintain that connection and return to it as necessary. It also helps explain how young people continue to need to make Mother's Day cards, for example, even though their mother may be no longer alive.

Among theories that examine styles of grief, the model developed by Stroebe and Schut (1999) is influential. It describes a model of loss and restoration orientation, in which these two are at opposite ends of a spectrum, with grieving young people oscillating between the two extremes. The 'loss orientation' is seen as the extreme that enables a young person to stay with the grief and focus on the pain and feelings in order to manage them; the 'restoration orientation' enables a young person to focus more on ways of dealing with loss by being practical, thinking of the future and perhaps not permitting the feelings to emerge. Stroebe considered that the most healthy form of grief is the one in which a young person is able to 'oscillate' between the two and not remain at either end of the spectrum for any length of time. This theory has influenced services such as those provided by Winston's Wish (a bereavement charity set up by Julie Stokes in 2004) and other organisations.

Research is constantly emerging that indicates the impact of bereavement on young people and how support can be shaped. These theories cover the many different aspects of bereavement and loss and form the basis of this book's approach. Knowing that the information and exercises within this book are based on sound, theoretical foundations (although new research is continually emerging), will be helpful to schools, carers and other professionals who wish to use the book to support bereaved teenagers.

In Conclusion

The developmental stage of adolescence is one of transition and, in conjunction with hormonal changes, influences profoundly the experience of bereavement and loss. The attachment history of the young person is also highly influential. Finally, the different theories of grief and bereavement help explain the different needs of adolescents.

Chapter 2
The Grief Process in Adolescence and its Implications

>Grief is not in vain,
>It's for our completeness,
>If the fates ordain
>Love to bring life's sweetness
>Welcome too its pain.
>
>Kath Walker (Oodgeroo of the tribe Noonuccal), 'Song', 1964

Differences between the Adolescent and Adult Experience of Loss

It could be said that, to a large extent, adolescents experience loss and death in the same way as adults. They are able to understand that death is permanent and they will have grief reactions in some form or another. They may at first deny that a loss has occurred, or they may become very angry or shocked that a person has left them. They will feel some form of shock, sadness and other feelings, and will probably feel these reactions deeply, and will need time to adjust to life without that person. If their loss is due to bereavement, it may take some time for them to move through the various stages of grief towards acceptance that the person has died and that their pain will often recur for many years. If the loss is from other causes, such as divorce or separation, or loss of the parent due to absence in military service or prison, the same stages of grief may occur, even though the ultimate outcome is not the permanent loss of an individual. It may, of course, feel as if the loss is permanent at the time.

However, the adolescent experience of grief and loss differs from that of adults in a number of significant ways.

Adolescents are not yet adults

They are dependant emotionally on those adults around them until at least the age of approximately 15 to 16 years. They are still forming their own personalities and reactions to life experiences. Therefore an experience of grief and loss at this age, whether from death or from other causes, is at first related to their prior experience of life within the family. It can and will shape their future perception of the world and, as such, is significant.

The support received from families, therefore, is vital. This is particularly the case if the loss is of a parent. In addition, the prior attachments to the person they have lost, especially if it is a bereavement, will affect their ability to express their grief openly and appropriately.

Implications

Adolescents will need to know that there is support available to them, either from school staff, family members or others. Existing relationships and styles of communication within the family home will become either an exaggerated version of what was present before, or the opposite, depending on the circumstances and personalities within the family. Young people who are preparing to leave home can sometimes decide to remain in the home and make very different life choices as a result of a significant loss, and the adults who support them, both families and professionals, can help them to make decisions that are helpful to their future needs.

If prior attachments between the young person and their carers or parents have been difficult, a member of the school staff can take on the role of trusted adult and listening ear, or a person to whom the young person can turn to if needed. Young people can choose to withdraw and become more insecure, or may become more outwardly confident and adventurous when faced with loss, and their need to have guidance and support can be heightened at these times.

Existing family attachments shape the adolescent experience of loss

As mentioned in Chapter 1, how secure adolescents are in their family relationships, how well bonded and attached they are to their caregivers, and how successful their parents or carers have been at offering secure attachment when younger, will all affect a teenager's response to loss. This is true of both adults and adolescents. However, the difference is that adolescence is a time of finally moving away from attachment figures in order to create a life and self of one's own. During this time attachment figures, whether mother, father, grandparents or other carers, become less significant on a daily basis and become 'internalised', meaning the memory of their attachment relationships informs their behaviour and future relationships. (See, for example, Holmes, 1993, for an explanation of this). When an adolescent experiences loss of any one of these figures, but especially a parent, there is an interruption to this process of moving to independence; the feelings aroused by loss are in direct conflict with their need to move away. Their need, once loss occurs, can be to remain close, retain memories, examine and explore very difficult feelings and experience loss. These feelings can call into question the person they had anticipated becoming in the future.

Implications

As a result of this conflict, adolescents can sometimes:

- regress to an earlier stage of development in order to create a sense of security and safety again, and attempt to heal any previous difficulties in their attachments;
- advance their development so that they jump straight to adulthood, taking on the sophisticated responsibilities normally associated with adulthood, but without some of the emotional maturity; or
- become stuck in the stage they are at when the loss occurs, which is one of an incomplete move towards adulthood, causing them to continue to be emotionally immature, perhaps rebellious or unable to create lasting and successful relationships.

It has been found that young people who have had successful attachment relationships from birth tend to feel their grief and loss deeply, but can move through their process of grief without becoming stuck in one of the above stages (Stokes, 2004). Therefore it can be important for young people who experience loss to recognise, if possible, the stage they are at, or for those nearby to help monitor if extra support such as that discussed in Chapters 3 and 4 could be of use. Although teenagers will respond in different ways to their experience of grief and loss, most will use all of the resources available, whether from peers, family or school, to survive and ultimately thrive.

Loss can set adolescents apart from their peers

This is particularly true if the loss results from a death, and can lead to feelings of isolation, bullying, or an inability to show grief openly within their peer group for fear of being different. Most of their friends will not have experienced a close family member dying, though some may have experienced separation or divorce, or be living in single-parent families. Adolescence is, however, a time of group identity, in which peers become significant, both as friends and as support at times of difficulty. One of the most significant aspects of bereavement or loss at this stage is therefore the feeling of being 'different'. This is a time when bullying can take place, when withdrawal from peers and other activities can occur, and when low self-esteem can manifest itself.

Implications

Due to their need to belong, adolescents can sometimes be forced into a position of pretending that their loss has not affected them, or that they are managing fine. Inwardly they could be very distressed, but they will not show it externally. Conversely, they can become more vulnerable and emotional, and decide to withdraw from their peers and remain wholly within the family. A third option, perhaps the most difficult, is when a young person appears to withdraw from both peers and family, and spend all of their time alone in their room or elsewhere. If professionals and family think this may be happening, it can be helpful to challenge a young person to talk to someone or find some other way to communicate their distress, as this level of isolation is one of the symptoms that can lead to more difficult responses to grief and loss as described in Chapter 3, 'How Adolescents Express Loss & How to Support Them'.

For this reason professionals may also need to monitor for bullying in particular or for other signs of isolation that can be a result of the experience of loss. (See also Toolkit and Resources)

Adolescents may express their feelings in different ways, or not at all

At first, when a teenager experiences loss, there may be the typical reactions of denial, anger and shock. These feelings are normal and associated with all types of loss. The adolescent experience is no different, but their feelings will probably manifest in different ways, depending on the nature of the loss, the age of the teenager and the family background. It would be typical for an adolescent to pretend that they are feeling fine when in fact they are not, as their natural inclination to withdraw from the family or close friends can be exaggerated by the experience of loss. Alternatively they could show their reactions by staying within the family home, rejecting their peers and withdrawing from their previous interests and activities.

Implications

It can be hard to know how a teenager is actually feeling, as they are often not sure themselves. They may not have the language to describe their feelings (as is the case with younger children), or they may be so shocked by their experience of difficult and overwhelming feelings that they are simply trying to avoid them. As the need to be part of their peer group can be overwhelming, this may overtake the need to acknowledge and express their feelings, even from quite a significant loss. For this reason, both professionals and family members may need to watch for signs that the young person is managing their loss appropriately, talking to someone, even if it is a friend, and that they are not becoming distressed without showing it. Signs of hidden distress can include disturbed sleep patterns, a young person who chooses to be out of the house at every available opportunity, or extreme changes in personality and behaviour. See also Chapter 3, 'How Adolescents Express Loss & How to Support Them', for more information.

Adolescents are still learning to manage their emotions

As most adolescents experiencing a significant loss will probably not have had any prior experience of this, the associated feelings can be particularly overwhelming. Adolescents often speak about their loss as the stage at which a new range of feelings entered their experience, and they will need time to know how to express these new feelings. However, they are not fully formed in their personality or response to life events yet, and will normally be at the cusp of deciding how they will live their lives as they grow older. A loss can therefore be a life-changing experience for them.

Implications

Whereas younger children tend to not question their reactions and show their feelings, adolescents will examine their reactions deeply and will need guidance and reassurance that what they feel is normal. Indeed, adults often need this support too, but adolescents, since they are already in the midst of a time of change and turbulence, have particular need for such reassurance. They will still need guidance on how to behave, what is appropriate, and how to express themselves. At times they still need the boundaries of timekeeping, appropriate behaviour and discipline.

The Stages of Grief

As grief develops, there are various stages that can occur and recur over time. None of these stages are linear, that is to say, they may not follow one another in a clear pattern at all, and some may come and go for a number of years. These stages may include the following:

1. Shock. This is a normal and typical reaction to loss, whether from bereavement or any other cause. The shock is the body's way of adjusting, as the news is often too great to bear and too difficult to accept. Shock can take many forms, but the usual form is a sense of unreality, a freezing of the reactions and numbness. There can also be strong feelings of both anger and sadness that come and go.

2. Mistrust that the loss has happened. Typically this follows on from shock and is part of the initial reaction about whether the loss can be accepted, whether the news is too great to take in, and a disbelief in the actuality of the loss, particularly if it is from bereavement, though feelings of loss resulting from separation and divorce can be equally as strong. An adolescent who still mistrusts the news will attempt to carry on life as normal, as if the person is still in their lives, perhaps going out as usual and ignoring requests to help in the house or to be involved in other daily activities.

3. Denial of the loss and a possible swing between denial and acceptance. Denial is a normal part of grief, and takes place as a young person swings between having to accept reality and not wishing, or being ready, to do so. Adolescents are no different from adults in this respect, except that their feelings are often heightened, so their sense of denial can also be heightened. Adolescents who are still in denial, but who are moving closer to acceptance of their loss, may begin to show deep feelings; however, they may also need time alone or may feel unable to talk about their loss. This can happen both before and after a funeral, and can happen at any stage of the loss, although it is more typical in the early stages, perhaps during the first few months.

4. Ultimate acceptance, often associated with deep feelings of mourning. As grief and loss are processes with no easy levels and stages, some adolescents will take many months, or even longer, to fully accept a loss. One of the reasons is that loss and acceptance bring with them

deep feelings, and feelings are not always easy for adolescents to accept or show. The length of time taken will depend on the personality, situation and circumstances of the loss.

5. Feelings of guilt, anger, sadness, fear, confusion and emptiness. These are the most common feelings associated with loss, but they can be accompanied by anxiety, numbness and other feelings. Adolescents will exhibit these feelings at different times and some will be stronger than others. They may not experience all of these feelings and some of the emotion may never fully be resolved, needing to be returned to later in adulthood. However, all adolescents experiencing grief and loss will have deep feelings at some stage during their grieving process.

6. Beginnings of the move towards gaining comfort from memories. Creating and retaining memories and being able to reminisce about their loved one allows a young person to move on with both their grief or loss and their life. Knowing that they have had someone important whom they have lost, although they may experience all of the pain, is reassuring for them as growing adults. By reaching this stage of their loss, young people are showing that they are able to face their future, holding within them the knowledge of their past. This stage can come either early or late in their grieving process, and should never be underestimated.

7. Acceptance that life can continue without the person they have lost. Adolescents, over a period of time, will accept that their loss has occurred and that they will never again be able to either see the person if they are bereaved or live as a complete family if the loss was from a separation or divorce. Once acceptance has been reached, adolescents will normally be able to fully focus on their stage of development again, although their mourning and feelings of grief may not cease and will certainly recur during anniversaries and significant events in their lives, such as marriage, the birth of children and similar.

8. Feelings of hopefulness for the future and a sense of gladness that the person was in their life. This stage can be reached once most of the other stages have been experienced. This assumes that the relationship to the deceased, or person who has left, was a reasonably successful one. Once this stage has been experienced, the teenager will almost always be able to adjust as a normal adolescent would to normal everyday experiences. Sometimes this stage is only reached when an adolescent becomes a young adult, due to the yearning they may have to return to the sense of safety and security they had before the loss occurred. Sometimes this stage is never fully reached. However, most of the time adolescents can feel this sense of hope for a future, and move towards adulthood successfully.

Anniversaries such as birthdays, the date of the death or loss, Christmas and other special occasions will nearly always bring back some of these feelings and responses.

Implications

Adolescents will need help to move through all stages of grief, and ultimately to the last stage, although the different stages may come and go over time. Their need as young people moving towards adulthood, however, will be to remember and store their memories, particularly if they have lost a parent through bereavement. Knowing that they can remember the person who has died can enhance their growth as they move through the various periods of their life. Most adults who have lost significant family members when young will speak of how the feelings never go away, but are triggered at times by the different stages of life as well as by anniversaries. They also speak of how important their memories are to their growing sense of themselves as adults.

> ## Case study
>
> Peter was 12 years old when his mother died from cancer after a very short illness. He remembered her being cared for by his father and that he tried to be helpful. He was an only child, so he and his father had to face the world together after her loss. He had previously been secure and happy, but her illness had rocked their world. School had helped at the time of the loss, and he had had time out before slowly returning to his school routine, where he found his peers and teachers sympathetic. He had supportive grandparents, and friends' mothers had also been there for him. He thought he was doing all right.
>
> He appeared to be coping well, slowly moving into the period of full adolescence, which he had entered just before she died. He was beginning to think of girlfriends and his future. However, when his father began a new relationship, he became very infantile and childish and, at the age of 14, he appeared to be very moody, not socialising much, not able to communicate how he felt, and his school marks began to deteriorate markedly. At first Peter's father thought it was just his age, but he became worried.
>
> His father tried to communicate with him about the new relationship, but Peter would simply shut down and not talk to him. After learning from school that Peter was not performing at all well, his father finally asked if he would like to see a counsellor at the agency that had supported them both during his mum's illness, and Peter agreed.
>
> During the counselling, Peter admitted that he was worried he was forgetting his mother, and had been having all sorts of difficult feelings he could not cope with, such as feeling angry and very, very sad, crying at night. He was very afraid that his dad's new partner would want him to call her 'Mum'. He also described how his dad had put away all their pictures of his mum, as the new woman in his life did not like

to see them. He was especially concerned about how their garden was changing, as there was a particular plant he had always felt was his mum's and which he tended lovingly as a memory, and now his dad was considering changing the garden completely. He was indeed grief-stricken all over again, due to this change.

Over time the counselling helped Peter accept that things did have to change, as his dad wanted someone else in his life, and that perhaps he could talk to his dad about the garden and the pictures. He eventually did so, and his dad was very understanding, and brought out again all the pictures he had put away. He also made Peter a long-lasting memory box for the pictures he particularly needed to have close to him. His dad had clearly not understood that Peter might respond so badly to such big changes, as he had been doing so well. Peter was slowly able to adjust to there being a new person in his dad's life, and his counselling helped him to rebuild his self-esteem and to manage his reactions to grief in a more mature way, so that he could once again enjoy being an adolescent.

Chapter 3
How Adolescents Express Loss & How to Support Them

> All things pass
> A sunrise does not last all morning
> All things pass
> A cloudburst does not last all day
> All things pass
> Nor a sunset all night
> All things pass
> What always changes?
>
> (Lao-Tzu [sixth century BC], from a translation
> adapted by Timothy Leary, *Psychedelic Prayers*, 1972)

Adolescent loss and grief is more similar to adult loss than to that of childhood grief, particularly in the later stages of adolescence, which is from the age of about 15 years. However, there are certainly some similarities to loss in childhood, particularly so when the young person's reaction is one of regression, a typical reaction to a shocking loss. Therefore this chapter includes some of the ways that the regressed adolescent who has returned to childhood expresses loss, as well as discussing those behaviours more typical of adolescents.

This chapter is divided into the following parts:

1. Physical reactions (mild and severe)
2. Emotional and psychological reactions (mild and severe)
3. Sleep issues and spiritual responses

Case studies are included to give examples and are based on actual cases, though with all identifying details changed. Suggestions for support are also discussed.

All adolescents will be helped by being given a time-out card (see the template in Resources) to use at school when needed. Making sure that there is a safe place for them to go, or a key person they can meet for five minutes if needed, will be a support for such young people. This can be helpful in all forms of response to loss, as it gives the young person permission to leave the everyday life of school for a short time. Most young people will recognise this need as being only temporary. It gives them the message that their needs and feelings are important and that they are listened to.

Physical Reactions to Loss (Mild)

Reacting physically to loss is a normal expression of grief in both adolescents and children, as well as in adults. It is an expression of the pain that we all feel on experiencing loss. Many who experience grief are surprised at how they are affected physically by tiredness and fatigue or other symptoms such as stomach pains or headaches. However, whereas children tend not to have the appropriate language to describe their reactions to loss and so physical symptoms allow them to express their feelings and responses, adolescents do have other options. Their brains are more developed, they can think more profoundly about their losses and they can be more analytical about how they feel. Mild physical reactions therefore are not of great concern, unless these are persistent, happen over a long period of time, and are not fully acknowledged by the parent or carer.

Stomach aches, headaches, tiredness, sickness and nausea are all typical reactions in grief and loss – all of these symptoms are a way of the body saying it has had a deep shock and is in pain. These symptoms may lead to lack of concentration, being unable to sleep or other reactions, but could be said to be very normal for a young person. The only time such symptoms should be a cause for concern is if they are excessive, have lasted for a long period of time, or appear to completely disable the young person and prevent them from leading a normal life for any length of time.

Suggestions for support

For young people who are experiencing mild physical symptoms, the main way to offer support would be to give a reassurance that this is temporary, to ensure they have attention from either their carers or professionals, and to give some acknowledgement of the pain of their loss. A time-out card can be given to temporarily support a young person who may be struggling with concentration at school as a result of these symptoms. In addition, checking that they are supported at home, and that they continue to take part in normal activities such as hobbies and seeing friends, can be of help. Suggested comments include:

> *I am really sorry to hear of your recent loss. It seems like it has caused a few problems for you with sleep problems/headaches, etc. I would like to assure you that this is normal for people experiencing such loss and with time these will disappear.*

You may feel that the pain/nausea is just one more thing to deal with after your loss, but it is actually your body saying you have had a lot to manage, so just let us know if you need some more support or someone to talk to.

Do let us know if you need some more time out or find it hard to concentrate as a result of your loss.

> **Case study**
>
> Adam was a 13-year-old who lost his mother to cancer after an illness of a year. He had a supportive father and a younger sister and had attended the funeral. He had appeared very brave at first, typical of boys his age, and had tried to check up on his father and sister. Then, within a month of his mother's death, he began to complain of sleep problems and also of regular headaches, particularly when at school. School had offered him a time-out card as soon as they heard of the bereavement, which he used occasionally. However, the headaches and sleep problems continued for another few weeks. As a result of the continuing sleep issues, which led to lack of concentration at school, his teacher contacted Adam's father to check if there was anything else they needed to know.
>
> His father was able to check how Adam was feeling and to offer other support, such as someone to speak to and the opportunity to talk more about their family loss. Adam's father had naturally been grieving himself, and had therefore missed some of the distress Adam had been feeling as he had not been showing any signs of his grief. It transpired that Adam's grief had finally arrived; he was distressed and needed simply to talk about his mum with his family and to visit her grave. He also said he did not like using the time-out card, and was trying to be 'normal' when his friends were nearby. His school spoke to him about it being fine to use the card, and asked if he would like a teacher to have a discussion with his friends, who wanted to support him. They also offered him one or two exercises from the Toolkit (see Chapter 5). As a result of this, Adam began to use the time-out card when he needed to, and he and his father were more open about how they felt about losing his mother. His headaches quickly disappeared and his sleep pattern gradually improved as he spoke more to his friends as well as his family. He had simply needed a few pushes in the right direction in order to manage his very difficult loss with the support of those around him.

Physical Reactions to Loss (Severe)

Persistent stomach aches or problems with eating, severe headaches or migraine, extreme fatigue or severe nausea and sickness can all indicate a more complicated reaction to a loss. Sometimes this reaction can be related to the cause of death, as with young people who feel pains in their stomachs after observing their sick parent with stomach pains. Shock can also cause such symptoms, the severity of which will depend on the length of time over which they have occurred, how extreme they are in relation to normal behaviour and how severely they affect normal everyday life. These reactions may also be the result of complex grief reactions connected to confusion or lack of information about the loss or death, a history of other losses, previous very complex family relationships or losses that are compounded by the most recent loss, or a build-up of tensions over time.

When a teenager reacts to loss with more compounded physical symptoms, this would normally indicate a deeper sense of loss and a more complex response that may take a little time to change. Although this can sometimes lead to an outside professional becoming involved, it would still be advisable to give an adolescent support from those around them. A more severe reaction that is expressed physically, if there are no other indications of complexity, can simply indicate the depth of distress that needs to be acknowledged. The general rule would be to say that a reaction is more severe *if it seriously interferes with normal life*.

There are a number of reasons why a young person may show more complicated responses to loss. These can include: the causes of the loss, such as a suicide or a sudden accident, which can be harder for a young person to understand and respond to; the nature of their relationship with the person they have lost, for instance a father they did not live with, which can cause complicated emotional reactions; the number of losses in their life, including divorce and other deaths, which could compound the effect of loss; living in a household in which the grieving adults are too deep in their own grief to be available emotionally to their young people; or they may be responding to the results of their loss due to a sensitive temperament. All of these factors can lead to a more complicated physical reaction to grief.

A note of caution – most professionals who offer emotional bereavement support for young people ensure that both the young person and related adults understand that this need for support is normally temporary and does not usually indicating an ongoing need. The aim is to avoid 'pathologising'; that is to say, making the reaction to the loss into an illness and a disease, rather than a temporary reaction to a difficult experience in life. Few grief reactions lead to permanent illness. However, with complicated reactions it is always important to consider counselling, art therapy or other forms of emotional and psychological help if the physical responses are seriously impairing a teenager's ability to thrive.

Suggestions for support

As with all reactions to loss that may be cause for concern, turning to the family first for their understanding of what is happening to the young person is important and valuable. Families normally know their young person best. Schools and other professionals will therefore need to be in close contact with a family if they perceive a young person with severe physical symptoms that are not being addressed. Attending a GP clinic is usually important with physical symptoms, to ensure that any other cause of physical pain is ruled out. This can also be helpful for more guidance on other support measures, such as assistance for nausea and sleeplessness.

The next option would be discuss with both the young person and their family why they think this may be happening now, and to offer some guidance or support to help them manage their physical responses. If the physical reactions are serious enough to warrant immediate attention, such as eating issues that have led to a young person showing signs of anorexia or bulimia nervosa, it should be recommended that the family visit their GP immediately if they have not already done so. Less severe responses, such as severe fatigue and withdrawal, can be supported with responses within school or by offering help from an external professional such as a counsellor or art therapist.

Families and professionals can also help the young person by linking the physical problems to the emotional cause, that of loss. Activities in the resource section of this book can be helpful. In addition, encouraging the young person to talk to friends, take up an activity such as a sport or other hobby that gives them an outside interest and helps to build self-esteem, and reminding them of activities they love, can all help when faced with young people whose distress is expressed physically rather than emotionally.

Other options include offering a time-out card. These are always valuable tools in helping a young person adapt to all aspects of loss, and teenagers who are experiencing severe physical symptoms will normally need time to adjust within the school environment as well as at home. Also helpful are offering a key person at school for the young person to go to whenever their physical reactions become overwhelming, and a family member who will spend more time with the young person, if possible, to help them adjust to severe losses such as those from accidents, complicated divorces and similar. Family support is always a key factor for young people, even older adolescents who are gradually moving from the centre of family life to a life as a young adult.

Case study

Deborah was a 12-year-old who was affected severely by the loss of her 15-year-old brother from cancer. She had lived with her sibling's illness for more than two years, but found it very hard to adjust once he died. She began to develop severe eating problems, not wishing to eat or being extremely fussy to the point where she would sometimes eat nothing all day. She also began to have severe problems with sleep. She showed a lack of concentration at school, and lost interest in her friends and her usual hobbies. School noticed her tiredness and her family told the school professionals of her issues with food. They observed, over time, a level of secretiveness and a loss of weight that gave them cause for concern.

The school finally contacted her family when Deborah appeared to become faint in class one day, and had spent another break time on her own. Deborah was asked what she wanted, which she had been asked before but had been unable to answer. This time she broke down and asked for help, although she clearly did not know what form that help should take.

The school and family together arranged for Deborah to see a professional who was able to diagnose the beginnings of an eating disorder and recommended counselling or art therapy for her psychological distress at her loss. The family were also involved in this psychological support, being encouraged to recognise that the nature of Deborah's loss, as her brother's sister, was different from the loss the rest of the family felt. They were able to access bereavement support for her and the other family members via the local children's hospice where her brother had died.

Over time, Deborah attended a clinic to help her with her eating, and the counselling she received helped her to talk about how her brother's illness and consequent death had affected her. She admitted she felt guilty that she was still alive when he was not, and that she felt she should have done more to help him. These were absolutely normal feelings that she needed to process so that she could grieve more appropriately. She also remembered many times when he had been sick physically, and she may unconsciously have wished to develop a similar symptom so she that she could understand how he had felt.

School gave her time out when she needed and sent work home so that she could remain involved in classes. Her friends visited her, as her family ensured that they felt welcome, which had been difficult during her brother's last few months. Her family reassured her that she had done nothing wrong, was much-loved, and that they did not want her to become ill. She eventually began to eat normally again, to sleep better, and to adjust to her severe loss, although her symptoms recurred for at least two years during the anniversaries of her brother's death and his birthday.

Emotional & Psychological Reactions to Loss (Mild)

Adolescents can have quite complicated emotional and psychological reactions to grief and loss, due to the stage of their emotional development. However, it is quite normal to show upset and distressed feelings due to a loss. It is also normal to show signs of regression to earlier stages of development, and to need parents and carers more than is usual for the adolescent's age. The following are a small selection of ways in which a young person may respond emotionally or psychologically to a loss, and which may indicate some need of support.

Sadness/upset

Young people may or may not be willing to show upset feelings to their peers, but feeling sad and upset is clearly a normal reaction to loss. Therefore if a teenager who has experienced any form of bereavement or loss shows these feelings fairly soon after that loss, this would be regarded as healthy. They may not always openly cry, but they may show signs, either in their physical demeanour or in their relationships to peers, that they are sad and low. They may also show their sadness by crying only with their family, only with their peers, or by choosing to cry alone.

Adolescents are at the developmental stage of transferring allegiances to their own age group; therefore if they have already transferred good, healthy attachments to their friends, including a girlfriend or boyfriend for older adolescents, it is quite normal for them to use this support to express sadness in this way. They will, of course, still need the support of their families. It can be hard at times for families to feel that they are no longer a significant support for their young people. However, it is quite normal that adolescents turn to their peers while the families support them at a distance.

Suggestions for support

Adolescents showing signs of sadness and upset will need simply to be reassured that their feelings are normal at times of loss and grief. At school it can be helpful to give a time-out card, offer them some time alone if they appear particularly upset, and check if they wish to be alone or if they would prefer company either from a friend or other adult they trust. Carers and parents can check how they are feeling and also reassure the young person that they can choose whether to talk, whether to be on their own, or how to express their feelings. Adolescents invariably like their own company at times, and of course in these days of the internet, social media and other social networks, they may well wish to gain comfort online with their virtual contacts.

It can be important to reassure young people that it is OK to cry as a result of a loss if needed, or to show signs of sadness, and that it is not a sign of weakness. You could say something such as:

> *I know you are hurting and sad as a result of your loss. You know it is OK to be sad? Just tell us if you need to go somewhere quiet or sit with someone for a while.*

For a young person who appears to be quite sad a lot of the time, knowing that it is normal to feel this way after a loss can be very helpful. Adolescents need to belong in their peer group, and knowing they are not alone with their feelings is therefore important. It can be helpful to say, for example:

> *I have seen you being sad at times, and perhaps it is helpful for you to know that others who have experienced what you have in losing someone important also feel like this. You may feel like you are the only one, and your feelings are really important, but sometimes it is important to know that other young people do feel like this. It is absolutely normal to feel like you do.*

This sort of reflection is particularly important for young people who have experienced little loss prior to their experience or who have had a sudden loss and therefore need reassurance that their feelings are normal. It is also helpful for young people who are feeling sad and showing signs of some isolation or withdrawal from their peers.

If the young person is both sad and showing signs of regression, a carer or parent could be more physically reassuring, giving or offering hugs and cuddles as this is a form of comfort which, though non-verbal, can be very supportive to young people who may be ashamed to feel so much younger than their years. Feeling sad is both difficult and, at times, frightening for young people who are beginning to become sophisticated emotionally, and it is therefore helpful to be reassured in different ways that crying and sadness are all acceptable.

Anger

Anger is another typical reaction to grief and loss, felt by most people, including adults and young children. Indeed, anger is a feeling more typical of adolescence than sadness, which can cause feelings of vulnerability at a difficult time of their lives. Anger can take many forms for young people, including being cross at something that would normally be easily accepted, or being slightly more irritable or frustrated than usual with their friends. They may be directly angry at the person who has died or gone away and wish to express this to their carers and peers. It may show as a 'short fuse' in their daily lives, and it is also possible for teenagers to turn their anger inwards onto themselves. Due to the stage of adolescence in which mood swings are typical, as a result of hormonal changes, parents and teachers can often become confused as to whether this reaction is 'just their age' or actually a reaction to grief. However, teenagers who show signs of anger, and who were previously not expressing these, can be presumed to be reacting as a result of their loss. It is important to note that adolescents who feel anger after a loss, but who were not previously angry, can become scared or shocked at their own reactions. In contrast, those who were already angry may actually show it less or escalate their anger to a higher level.

Suggestions for support

There are a number of ways to support young people who have angry reactions to loss, depending on how they express their anger, their age range, and also the cause of the loss.

First, it is important to reassure a young person that being angry is one of the most normal feelings in grief and loss, and that their feelings are not unusual. This can be reassuring and also help at times to calm the feelings of anger. Second, the type of support will depend on how the anger is expressed, though of course expressing it in an out-of-control or destructive and violent way is not acceptable. Young people can be given suggestions about how to find a safe outlet for their anger, such as sports, or listening on earphones to loud music, if they appear to be struggling with this. See the Toolkit activities for help with expressing anger. You could, for instance, say:

> *It seems like you are angry at the moment, and it is important for you to know that being angry is a normal part of feeling grief and loss. What you have been through is hard for you, so let's think of ways you can be angry without disturbing others or taking it out on them.*

It can also be important that both professionals and parents acknowledge that a young person is showing their feelings of loss through being angry or frustrated, as when a young person feels 'heard' in this way, it can help the process of loss and can even reduce the feelings. Things to say include:

> *We want you to know how we notice you are angry at the moment and just want to remind you that you can talk to us whenever you need to.*

> *It's OK to be angry, as what you have experienced is difficult, so just let us know if you need to go away and get angry, or are feeling more tense at times. We can offer you some time out if you need this.*

Carers can say, for example:

> *We still need to live together, but strong feelings like anger need to be let out. So perhaps going to your room and playing music, or kicking a football outside when you really feel angry might help – or perhaps you could talk to us about what is making you particularly angry?*

Carers and parents may find it difficult to have an angry teenager in the house, but responding with support and reflective comments, plus helping the young person to be angry without taking it out on other family members, can be helpful for all in a grieving process.

At school, anger is also not easily acceptable, as discipline and rules are important. However, a young person being angry as a result of a loss is not something easily ignored. It is always better to talk to the young person and negotiate first, rather than making rules and then expecting them to be adhered to. As the young person will be in pain and grief as a result of their loss, from whatever cause, try and approach them in a discreet way and offer support and a place to go if, for example, their anger is becoming more disruptive.

> *I notice that one of the ways you are showing your loss is by being angry – although school is not the easiest place for this, as we have rules that cannot be changed. We want you to know that we are not going to try and stop you being angry, but we would like you to use the time-out card so you can find a safe place to be, or go to speak to [name of key person] if you need to let off some steam. We find this really helps when young people are affected, as you are, by their loss.*

If a young person is showing signs of anger and is normally never angry openly, it can be helpful to reassure them that it is as a result of their loss and is usually temporary. Saying something can be helpful, such as:

> *It can feel scary to show anger when you don't normally do this. But just remember that your feelings are as a result of your loss, and that others around you will understand. Sometimes when people experience the sort of loss you have had, strong feelings simply have to be expressed, and your grief is coming out this way.*

> *If you feel you are particularly angry or on a short fuse, let us help to find ways for you to express it, such as sports or listening to loud music, as there are plenty of ways to let out anger without hurting yourself or others. We can also suggest some activities if you like.*
> [See Toolkit, 'Anger: Wild Animals Drama', and 'The Shape of My Anger', for examples of activities that might be used.]

When a young person is turning their anger inwards, they can show this through being cross with themselves for work they have done badly, by blaming themselves in some way for the loss, or by becoming very tense but unable to express this at all. They can even show the beginnings of self-harming behaviour, such as starting to smoke if they have not done so before. Self-harm does not necessarily mean that a person does physical harm to their body with an object. However, these are mild forms of self-harm and the usual way to help would be to encourage the young person to recognise that they actually feel angry and then to offer help with ways to express it that do not harm either themselves or others. It may be possible to say, for example:

> *I have noticed you seem to blame yourself a lot at the moment/have taken up smoking/ [other], and wonder if this is to do with how you feel about your recent loss. Sometimes when people do this, it means they are actually angry but have no way of expressing*

this – I wonder if this is true for you? And, if it is, would it be helpful to talk to someone/ do an activity/take some time out sometimes?

Always remember that adolescents are developmentally at a time of change, and for this age group an extra change such as loss can cause severe emotional reactions. Anger, although not always acceptable, is normal within grief and a young person who understands this and manages to express it without upsetting others, or hurting themselves or others, will probably be able to adjust to their loss better than those who do not.

Case study

Brian was a young man of 14 when he experienced the loss of his stepfather, who had brought him up for most of his life. His stepfather had suffered a serious lung disease that had affected him for the last few years of his life, so that Brian and his older sister had been part-time young carers during the final two years. Added to this, his mother had experienced mild depression for some of Brian's early life, during the time of her break-up with his birth father, with whom he had no contact. However, Brian had appeared to be a well-adjusted young man who was beginning to mature and had just had his first girlfriend.

Brian began showing signs of being quite angry within three months of the loss. At first he continued to support his mum, who was devastated by the loss of her second husband. His sister also supported him and their mother. However, as his grief really began to emerge, the prime feeling was clearly anger and outrage that he had lost a second father, the first having simply disappeared. At home he became more irritable and difficult to communicate with. At school he began to get into trouble for having fights and for answering teachers back, something he had never previously done.

The school had been very supportive of him when they first heard about his stepfather's death, offering him a time-out card, some counselling if needed, and a key worker if he ever needed to talk. However, he had not wanted this at the time. They were therefore surprised to get a phone call from his mum saying how worried she was about his behaviour, and asking whether they could they offer him extra support. As a result of this, his year head spoke discreetly to him about how he was doing, and asked if he would now like the time-out card. Brian was also asked if there was a particular staff member he felt he trusted enough to go to and talk about how he was feeling. As there was not, he was offered a counsellor/art therapist and he agreed to go, since he was beginning to realise for himself that he was getting more upset and angry than he had ever been before. He had begun to fall out with his mates, and didn't seem to enjoy any of the things he used to, such as football and computer games.

> In the counselling Brian was helped to learn about his anger and how to let it out safely. His friends were helped by some group activities based on loss (see Toolkit, 'Anger 4: a Story of Loss', for example), and he used his time-out card when he needed to. The seeds of his anger had actually been sown before his step-dad had become ill, at the time when his birth father had left and not kept in touch with them. The counselling therefore helped him to make sense of those previous losses, and gave him time to adjust to them without letting his anger become more embedded in his character.

Clinginess/insecurity

Older adolescents may not show any sign of clinginess openly, perhaps because they feel they are too old to do so. Younger adolescents, however, may need to regress and can become insecure as a way of showing their grief or loss, just as younger children do. Certain teenagers will therefore need more reassurance from those around them, particularly their carers, and this is a normal response to loss, whatever the cause. If the loss was sudden and unexpected, the shock of this can cause quite severe regression and withdrawal for a time, with young people needing reassurance that their life will remain as normal as possible and that their family will support them.

Sometimes clinginess in adolescents will cause a young person to stay at home more, rather than go out with friends. Teenagers can also become more physically clingy, a stage they may have previously left, and may show this by sitting closer to their carers or even teachers, or need more hugs and cuddles again from family. This is quite normal and can be very reassuring for adolescents at the early stages of loss and grief if they choose to remain close to their home base.

Older adolescents may show insecurity in different ways. It may manifest in them becoming the person who cares for the adults around them, in an attempt to protect them from harm and danger. They can also show insecurity by withdrawing from contact with their peers and just wishing to be with their families, again a normal reaction in the early days of grief and loss.

Suggestions for support

Adolescents who show a tendency to regression or clinginess, however it is expressed, are asking for signs from their carers that life will remain safe and consistent despite their losses. They are also adjusting to what is a change of situation within their family, which could lead to them having a different role: for example, being the only male or female left behind, or becoming the eldest sibling rather than the middle one. This can lead them to question how they perceive themselves in the family and a period of adjustment is important. Support that enables a young person to remain feeling safe and to understand their new role within the family can therefore be important. Carers may wish to say things such as:

We know how important the family is to you at the moment. Don't worry if you want to stay in more than usual, that's fine. And we can talk together if there is anything happening you don't like or understand.

I realise how everything has changed. It must be very confusing for you, just let us know if there is anything you want to talk about or any questions you may have.

Some encouragement about asking any questions they may have is important, as is reassurance that some things will not change and that their choices are acceptable (for example, wishing to stay in rather than go out with friends). Sometimes just a hug is enough. Teenagers can respond well both to being listened to and having open discussions to find out how they feel, when prompted in the right way. Both at home and at school adults can offer time to talk and listen, saying such things as:

Please do let us know whenever you want to talk, or to understand the things you are going through and how you are now. We/your family want what is best for you and talking can sometimes help. We will listen and not judge if things need to be said.

Alternatively some of the exercises in the Toolkit can help them to express themselves, as some teenagers will find it hard to say anything at this time. They may need either to listen, or to talk and to know that their carers or teachers have noticed their behaviour. This then opens a dialogue for them to explore what is best and to help with their feelings when they are ready.

Allowing such young people a time-out card can be very beneficial, as it gives them time to adjust if the daily life of school becomes too busy, or if they suddenly become upset and feel they need their carer but cannot say anything. These feelings are normal in adolescence and, of course, are compounded because the teenager is no longer a young child who can ask for their parents.

For carers, it can sometimes feel hard to approach adolescents who may previously have begun to withdraw and spend more time alone or with their peers. However, if you remember that inside they may be feeling lost and alone, but have limited ways to show this due to their age, this can give you the confidence to approach your young people. It is best to remember that saying something can often be better than saying nothing. Making a tentative offer of support or a reflection on how they may be feeling, could be all they need to respond.

For professionals, similarly, reminding ourselves that these adolescents are still young children inside, particularly at a time of loss, can help tentative approaches in offering support. It is fine to say such things as:

I have noticed that you are staying in your room more, even when [name of friend/loved one] contacts you. I wonder if you want to talk about this, as it may be to do with your recent loss?

I am wondering if the reason you want to look after me all the time is because it is scary to think that someone has died/gone to prison/[other]? I know how much you care, but you are a young person and your life is important too.

If the teenager simply wants more physical reassurance, telling them that this is fine can be very important, as it allows them to go through this phase of loss. Carers could say:

I know that normally you don't like to be so physically close these days, but I wonder if it is important now, and I will give you as many hugs as you need to get you through this time.

For a teacher or other professional to recognise that adolescents are less confident can be equally validating. This can be done by saying such things as:

I wonder if at the moment it is harder to be strong, as you have experienced the loss of [name of loved one] and we are happy to support you with extra time, support from your friends, or [other support].

Adolescents are at a time of transition, therefore enabling them to face this phase of insecurity and regression can help them return more quickly to the actual experience of moving beyond childhood to adulthood. A temporary regression or feeling of insecurity can normally be overcome with time and support.

As with all these reactions, if the symptoms persist for any length of time and are excessive, particularly if it is noted that the young person's everyday life is being inhibited, this can be said to be a more complicated reaction to loss.

Fear/anxiety

In a similar way to clinginess, adolescents quite naturally can have fears associated with their loss, some real, some imagined. If a parent has died, young people can fear that their remaining parent will also die. If they have lost a sibling, their fears may be compounded by the loss of their role within the family, such as the change from being one of a pair of siblings to being the only one. They may fear that they could also die. Loss due to separation or divorce can cause the fear, for example, that they will lose contact with one of their parents, or have to move house or school. If a parent or older sibling has gone away on military service, the very real fear that they may die is also present.

Young people who feel fear and anxiety as a result of their loss will often not show this openly. However, they may show their anxiety in their behaviour or attitudes, for instance not being able to concentrate on schoolwork, withdrawing from normal social activities, or monitoring closely how their parents or carers are managing. These young people may be feeling fear due to their loss and they need reassurance that their fears (including perhaps irrational or unanswerable fears, such as the fear that the world will come to an end, or more familiar fears, such as worrying their parent will die) will not come to pass.

They may also be feeling anxiety, which can inhibit even daily needs such as eating and sleeping. Fears such as these stifle the normal behaviours and interests of young people. It can therefore be helpful for them to explore their fears and anxieties, and perhaps either name them or find another way to express them so that they are reduced in impact. The Toolkit offers suggestions for support to help young people who are struggling with their fears and anxiety.

The impact of fears and anxieties on adolescents can be quite profound, and can lead to differing behaviours, including withdrawal or excessive care of the parent left behind. Fear may also cause the young person to try to become a parent figure, either to their siblings or to their own mother or father, as a way of filling a gap in their family. They may have nightmares or seem withdrawn. If their loss is from separation and divorce, teenagers may not wish to show their reactions and fears, as they may not want to upset either parent. This can sometimes lead to secrecy or going out more, as a way to prove that everything is normal. Being reassured that these fears are simply fears and are not real, or that they will be told if any significant change is likely to take place, can usually help.

The most significant way to help teenagers who are showing fear in some way is to maintain lines of communication, to give support either by talking or reassurance, and to help with understanding that their fears are temporary or will be fully taken into account when referring to the future. Fears can inhibit young people in their relationships with their peers, and can block a sense of self-worth and affect levels of self-esteem. So it is important to support these young people.

Suggestions for support

Adolescents, in particular, will benefit from being told what is happening and when, who will be looking after them, where they will be living and what role they can now play in supporting the family. They like information, opportunities to ask questions, involvement in all aspects of family life and a level of control over their own life and environment. As their need is to feel secure again, many adolescents will benefit from having someone who they can turn to if they feel especially fearful, and this can be, for example, a friend, family member, member of school staff, or counsellor. A pet or even a toy can also fill this role, even for older adolescents. Saying such things as:

> *We want you to know you can ask us anything; we will always tell you what is happening and if you need extra support, just ask.*

If you want to go out, or spend more time at home, that is fine. We know that at times like this it is tough being a teenager, but we want you to know that we hope life can go on as normally as possible, and that you can still see your friends, go out and have fun. But if you need your family, we are here for you.

It is helpful to give them time to talk about anything to do with the loss, but also the option to find their own ways to cope with it. When they are showing signs of having fears and anxieties, they may need particular reassurance that their fears are not going to be realised, such as fearing the loss of another family member. Giving them space to say how they feel and to have time alone with their friends or doing other activities, can give them a sense of normality when things are changing, particularly if their loss is from death. It would also be typical for a teenager never to openly say that they are scared or worried, as this could be seen as a sign of weakness at this age. However, they may show their fear in different ways, such as those described above, remaining close to home, refusing to see friends, or changing other behaviours. They can also show their worry through having difficulties sleeping.

Helpful things to say can include reminding them they can talk at any time, that you care and that it is all right for people to have unusual feelings when they experience loss. Other ways to support could be by reassuring them that they can see their friends and do normal things if it is helpful, and encouraging them to find a role in the family. Professionals can say such things as:

I wonder if you need to talk. If you do, remember to ask [the person allocated] for some time.

We understand that something difficult has happened, so if you find it hard to say how you feel, just use your time-out card or bring a friend with you to talk to us.

We know you have experienced a difficult loss and there is no shame in having feelings as a result of this. So let us know if we can help.

Changes of personality and behaviour (e.g., from extrovert to introvert)

Quite often when a young person first loses someone they love, they will respond in chaotic ways that are not typical of their usual personality. They may therefore become more quiet or withdrawn and wish to spend less or even more time with their friends. Alternatively, they may also become more animated, over excitable and extrovert. This is generally a typical reaction to loss. Both adults and adolescents take time to adjust to loss, and this is one way in which the disorientation that is felt when a loved one dies can show itself. Losses from other causes can also require a level of adjustment leading to changes of apparent behaviour.

Adolescents, however, are in the early stages of character formation, and are often still creating their own identity and personality, particularly in the early teens. It could be said, therefore, that an experience of loss, especially a serious loss such as the death of a parent or sibling, can have a profound impact on this work of 'becoming' someone. Many adults will talk of how the loss of an important person in their lives when they were younger helped shape both their character and their choices in life. It is important to support young people (who are already in a phase of personality and character formation) through the extra transition brought about by loss, so that they are able to continue to develop and incorporate the lessons learnt from their loss experience.

Suggestions for support

Simply acknowledging the changes of personality and reactions that are expressed can be important for a young person. If the changes are affecting their friendships, for example, it may be important to check if the teenager simply needs to have some time alone or with their family before returning to their friends. Alternatively, they might have made a conscious decision to no longer see certain friends, as an experience of loss can help them reassess their values and this can include friendships.

Another way that changes can affect young people is in their choice of activities. A young person who becomes extroverted after previously being introverted or quiet may find they are exploring many different avenues, such as new sports or different hobbies. Sometimes this is very appropriate and helpful for them, and sometimes it is a way of escaping their real feelings of pain. Support for such young people could involve helping them to review their choices and perhaps talking these through with someone, such as a trusted friend, family member, school staff member or counsellor.

When talking to young people who are showing changes in either personality or choices they are making, it could be helpful to say such things as:

> *We have noticed you are changing at the moment. I guess this is because of the losses you have experienced. We just want to check that you are happy with these changes, as sometimes we change without knowing why, and sometimes we are not happy with these changes. If you need someone to talk to while these are happening, just let us know.*

> *We want you to know we support you whatever you do. However you do appear to be changing personality and choosing such different things to do, and we need to check if you are all right with this. Is it making you happier? If it is, that is fine. If it is not, we can always help you to think through which choices you really want to stick with and which are not really you. I guess these choices are because of the recent losses, but just let us know if this helps.*

Case study

Anne was a 14-year-old girl who had previously been very committed to her schoolwork and was quietly ambitious, diligent and hardworking, while having a small, good peer group. She had had a happy life in her home with her mother, father and younger brother.

When she experienced a sudden change of home life due to her parents separating, she underwent a change of behaviour and interests. Her mother described her personality as moving from one of being easy-going and happy to being challenging and pushing all the boundaries, including those of timekeeping and friendships. She began to get poor marks at school and mix with different friends, who went out more at night and were more 'wild'. Teachers noticed her being more resistant to discipline and often looking tired. As this coincided with a greater emphasis on exams in her GCSE years, the teachers at first thought it was due to the stress and attempted to support her academically. However, after a consistent period of low marks, rudeness to teachers and what appeared to be a complete change of personality, they contacted her mother.

After a meeting the school realised that Anne's behaviour was due to the changes in her home life, as she had been close to her father and was still upset that her parents had separated. Her father had left the family home, and Anne and her brother were only seeing him occasionally. The school offered Anne a time-out card and asked her if she would like to speak to someone, either a counsellor or a member of staff she trusted. With the encouragement of her mother she agreed to see a counsellor. She also began to use the time-out card to speak to the pastoral head on a casual basis. Anne was able to reflect on whether the choices to change her friends and not to do her schoolwork were in her best interests. She also acknowledged that she was angry and confused about the separation. She had taken her 'father's side' and so felt a stranger in her own home.

With the help of counselling, talking and completing some exercises on emotions (see Toolkit, 'A Collage of Feelings', and 'Anger: Moulding My Anger', for example), Anne was able to talk to her mother about the separation, and review contact with her father. Her work gradually improved. She did, however, choose to remain in contact with her new circle of friends, and became a more sociable party-going teenager. She realised that she wanted to keep some of the changes brought about by the separation.

Emotional & Psychological Reactions to Loss (Severe)

Sometimes adolescents have more complex reactions to their loss, psychologically or emotionally. This may be due to a previously complicated family history, previous losses, or because of something they have seen or experienced that has affected them more profoundly. It can also be related to their personality and new events in their life. Young people can react strongly to severe loss (such as losing a parent) when more normal events such as moving home, conflicts with step-families, moving to a different class, losing a close best friend or ending a relationship occur at the same time as the major loss.

However, unlike younger children, the complex reactions which adolescents express are complicated by their stage of emotional development, as they are growing towards adulthood and away from their childhood, but needing to remain attached to their families. As a result of the complex effects of loss for this age group, adolescents can show extreme emotional reactions such as withdrawal or aggression, but they may also hide other serious reactions. These can include: risk-taking behaviour, such as taking alcohol or drugs or driving fast cars; becoming over-sophisticated in an effort to manage their feelings, often taking on an adult role in a family to replace the lost person; and developing more serious mental health issues such as depression, anorexia or bulimia nervosa, or self-harming behaviours, mild or severe.

These last, severe, problems may be well hidden from those around them, which means that adolescents are a more vulnerable group when it comes to reacting to severe loss. For this reason it is necessary to pay close attention to those young people who may have experienced more than one loss or who are more vulnerable emotionally due to previous life history or character, especially when they are showing extreme feelings or showing no signs of distress at all.

Support for these adolescents can include gaining their trust, perhaps by listening to them and giving them opportunities to express how they feel safely. It can be advisable to give them the independence to see their friends in a safe environment, perhaps inviting them into the home, while remaining aware of the normal forms of discipline such as time boundaries. As teenagers often have mood swings, keeping lines of communication open is vital. Carers can reassure them that they are loved, whatever they say or do, and offer them space to ask questions, talk more openly and discreetly offer physical reassurance. Professionals can help by asking if there is a trusted adult they would like to talk to or spend some time with when they are feeling distressed, and can give a time-out card that can be used with a friend if needed. The more a young person trusts adults nearby, the more they will begin to show their true feelings and perhaps not develop more extreme reactions.

Extreme feelings

Adolescents can manifest more significant reactions to loss that may be expressed by continuous crying and sadness, or extreme and constant anger or irritation. The feelings of young people stuck in this reaction to loss have become all-consuming, and this can inhibit all other aspects of normal life, such as concentration on schoolwork, having fun with friends, hobbies or family life. Although this reaction could be normal at various stages of a more complicated loss, such as the sudden loss of a close relative or the suicide of a parent, constant, ongoing signs of intense emotion are a sign of a young person needing extra support. Adolescence is already a stage of heightened emotions due to hormonal changes and other developmental changes, and this can be seriously exacerbated by a severe loss.

Suggestions for support

One of the first ways a young person can be supported is by offering them space to tell someone how they feel, even though this may seem obvious. This should be done discreetly, for example, not in front of their peers and at a time that is not usually taken up with other activities. A break time or lunch can be the most appropriate. Saying such things as:

> *I have noticed you looking a bit low/showing some signs of strong feelings and wondered if you would like to talk to someone, either myself or someone else, about this?*

This gives the young person both an indication that they have been noticed and also an offer of extra support if needed. It would be quite typical, however, for a teenager to refuse this offer, and so it could be followed up, if necessary, a few days later with another conversation such as:

> *Do you remember I asked how you were doing the other day? Well, I notice things don't seem to have changed, and wanted to remind you that the offer is still there. If you like, you can bring a friend with you or get your parent/carer to speak to me.*

This then gives the young person further options, if needed. Obviously, if they still appear distressed and this is definitely affecting their work at school or their peer relations, it may be time to have a full discussion about contacting their parents or carers to support them. But sometimes an approach such as this will be welcomed, as the young person may be desperate for someone to talk to about their experience of their loss.

If a counsellor is available in school, it is also helpful to offer this specifically, as you are showing that you believe they would benefit from this, and that you are taking their feelings seriously. Many young people will have preconceived ideas about counselling and art therapy, unlike younger children who are usually more open to these ideas. It is important, therefore, to make the offer in a way that is discreet, respectful and describes what the counselling can offer. For example:

I wonder if you know there is a person available at school who you can talk to privately if you would like to? None of your friends need know that you are going to them, and they will keep whatever you say private, unless of course you tell them about being seriously hurt by someone. Sometimes when a person has experienced the sort of things you have, it can help to talk to someone out of the situation. Would you be willing to try it?

It is never helpful to force a young person to see a counsellor if they do not wish to, but giving them options, reminding them that conversations are private and confidential within limits, and that their friends do not need to know, can help them make a decision to try it.

Of course, a young person who has experienced a loss, from any cause, may not wish to speak to anyone. However, if they are showing serious signs of distress, and this is definitely affecting them in their schoolwork and their friendships, even if the family are unaware of it, a school professional can be significant in offering them the support they need.

Counselling is one option, but art therapy or drama therapy are further possibilities in some schools. Offering this form of support to a young person does not mean that there is something seriously wrong with them; all professionals who offer support to those experiencing loss will agree that this is purely emotional and psychological support and does not mean the young person has a mental health issue. The aim of professionals in this field is not to 'pathologise' grief or loss. Only very occasionally does mental illness stem from serious loss. Counselling or art therapy at this stage can help to prevent more serious issues later in life, however, and, given the stage of life of adolescents, it can be very timely.

Other ways to offer support for young people showing extreme emotions are by offering a time-out card, by offering to talk to their parents or carers, suggesting some of the exercises found in the Toolkit, or by using *Rory's Story* (Jacobs, 2014), the book accompanying this workbook, which has exercises and prompts throughout.

Extreme withdrawal

Just as with a show of extreme emotions, teenagers who appear to be extremely withdrawn, particularly if there has been a change in character and they were previously well engaged with their peers and their work, are showing signs of more severe distress. It can be easy to overlook those who are withdrawing as they will not wish to draw attention to themselves and will perhaps be much quieter in lessons, on their own in breaks, or less engaged in all activities. Depending on their age and stage at school, they may also show erratic school attendance. Just as with those who are showing their feelings outwardly, however, these young people are showing their distress, but without wishing to 'make a fuss'.

They may be depressed or prone to mood swings, which can be exacerbated by their age and their personal experience of loss. They may also be in severe denial or pain internally, but have no way of showing it outwardly, again due to their age. This type of behaviour in adolescents who have experienced loss can be particularly difficult to spot at times, as these young people will attempt to 'hide' at school and not wish to speak at home. It is therefore particularly important that family, friends and professionals be alert to the needs of this group.

Suggestions for support

For these young people it will be particularly important to be very discreet when offering support, as what they are saying in their behaviour is that they do not wish to be disturbed. However, they are also saying that they do not know how to ask for help and a professional such as teacher or teaching assistant could be just the right person to help them find words for what they need. They may also need a more experienced mental health professional such as a counsellor or art therapist if their withdrawal is so extreme that it is leading to other behaviours, for instance the beginnings of self-harm.

It can be very hard for such young people to admit they can benefit from extra support. However, parents in particular, or a close trusted friend or teacher may be able to approach them to try and have a conversation, saying such things as:

I am sorry to disturb you but I am really concerned about how quiet you are – do you mind me asking, are you OK, and would you like to tell me about it?

This is very direct and to the point, often helpful when a young person is withdrawn and possibly full of thoughts and feelings that are waiting to come out. Similarly, if you have a counsellor or art therapist in the school, offering a meeting with them can be helpful, again very directly, saying for example:

I wonder if you know there is a counsellor/art therapist in the school. As I have noticed you being so very quiet, meeting with someone like that could help you tell someone what is going on without anyone passing judgement. You have had something difficult happen to you, and it is not surprising if you are struggling, and this is exactly why we would like to offer the counselling to you.

If counselling is not available in school, and there is no one else suitable, it would be good to offer the resources that other local agencies can supply.

Families can consider if they need to reach out and speak to a young person who is keeping to themselves. This can be done discreetly, perhaps offering some quality times together, either for sharing memories, or simply checking how they are. It can sometimes be hard to approach such young people, but it is helpful not to overlook the person who is quiet and hidden in their bedroom all evening, or going out quietly without telling anyone. You could say:

We know you just want to be left alone, but we want you to know that we are here for you if you ever need to talk. And if you don't want to talk to us, have you considered talking to someone else like a counsellor, or even someone else in the family?

We have noticed you seem so quiet and withdrawn and are worried about you. Is there anything we can do to help? Would you like to have someone to talk to about it – us or someone else? We know how difficult the past few months have been and want you to know you are not alone.

Case study

Sarah was a 13-year-old who lost a much-loved grandfather and then her father in quick succession, her father from cancer and her grandfather from heart problems. This was compounded by the fact that her mother and her father had been in the process of separating, and he had been living separately for the last year of his life. He had already moved out, but moved back in so that Sarah's mum could look after him for the last two months. Sarah had one younger brother.

Sarah began to show signs of serious withdrawal over a period of two months, some four months after her father died. At first she had appeared fine and was continuing with school and activities. But she then withdrew and began not to go out with friends, to stay in at breaks at school and her school marks deteriorated rapidly. Teachers became concerned when she began to have erratic attendance over a period of a month, and Sarah continued to be absent on a regular basis although her mum promised to make sure she came to school.

School arranged a meeting with Sarah and her mum. Sarah was unable to say anything at this meeting, though her mum did say that she had begun to spend all her time in her bedroom and she was concerned about some of her internet sites. When school offered a counsellor to support Sarah, she seemed horrified.

However, Sarah's mum later discovered that one of the websites Sarah had viewed was a suicide pact site. This finally became the catalyst for Sarah and her mother to talk, as the discovery was so shocking. As a result of their conversation, in which Sarah admitted her deep distress, her mother insisted they both go to the GP and let school know that she had finally begun to talk. The GP was able to refer Sarah to the local Child and Adolescent Mental Health Services (CAMHS) who arranged a series of therapy sessions due to her suicidal thoughts. School was then able to follow this up with a regular counsellor, which she agreed to, and Sarah began to talk more openly to her mum about the loss they had experienced as a family.

> As a result of the support Sarah received, she slowly began to share her fears and talk to family and friends. Sarah was gradually able to express her own grief and loss, and make sense of the nightmares and confusions she had experienced. She began to go out with friends again within about six months of the first therapy session, and to attend school regularly.

Risk-taking behaviours

When a young person shows signs of taking risks, such as drinking alcohol to excess or staying out very late, driving fast cars or mixing with a dangerous group of people, such as a gang, the message they are giving is that they are trying to make sense of their lives and they do not know how to do so. If a young person has begun this behaviour as a direct result of a significant loss, rather than as a part of their growing up and exploration of life, they can be assumed to be struggling emotionally. It may be that such young people have lost trust in the adults who care for them or teach them, or that they believe by acting in this way they will feel better. It is normal, even in adulthood, for people to choose activities that distract them from feeling pain, and in these cases, the adolescents are choosing such behaviour as it gives them a thrill that is the very opposite of the pain they are feeling underneath. It is not surprising therefore that many adolescents do explore risk-taking at some stages of their development. It is when the risk-taking is extreme, all-consuming and is clearly stopping the young person from functioning as they used to, that extra support is needed.

Suggestions for support

It can be very difficult to support young people if they are determined to take risks. However, there are some options for both professionals and carers that may prove helpful. Professionals can attempt to engage with the teenager and find someone they may trust to talk to, allowing them time to recover if they have had a serious loss such as a parent die from suicide or similar. Directing young people to other agencies where they may meet similar young people can be very helpful. It is useful to have a list of local agencies within a bereavement policy, and these can include both agencies directly supporting young people with loss, and other counselling agencies. Being given a time-out card, and having permission to not attend all classes can be helpful, providing the young person does not take advantage of this. Being directed to a sports activity or drama class so that they can express themselves in a non-verbal but physical way can also be extremely helpful for such young people.

A young person who chooses a risk-taking approach to their loss can often be in trouble in school. If this is the case, it can be possible to use detention or day exclusion as a means of supporting them, offering activities during the detention, or the chance to speak to someone about their loss. Exclusion can also be useful for carers and schools to offer a combined approach to support; carers can spend quality time with teenagers in an attempt to engage their trust and schools can show the impact of their risk-taking behaviour and its implications if they do not change. It can be helpful to say such things as:

We know you have had a difficult time recently, due to your loss. We wonder if there is another way of managing this without getting into trouble. Would you like to speak to someone/for us to speak to your parents/carers, or to have a regular meeting with you. We can allocate a tutor for you to go to when you need to let off steam during a school day if that will help. We do not like to see young people like you fall behind and get into trouble for something that is not their fault. And what happened to you was not your fault.

You can remind them that they have a future ahead of them and that they can choose what that might be, saying for example:

It makes us very sad to see you in trouble at this time. You do still have a good future ahead of you if we could support you in getting to it. What is it you would really like to do when you are older?

This has the added advantage of both helping a young person focus on something ahead of them and perhaps distracting them from their current pain.

The most significant issue for a young person who is choosing risk-taking behaviour, is for them to find just one trusted adult they can turn to. If they can do this, it is often possible for them to move beyond this phase of grief and loss and begin to express their feelings in a more appropriate way. Both schools and carers can try to identify someone the young person could begin to trust. Unfortunately it is rarely the parents or carers themselves, simply because of the nature of the teenager's stage of development, but it could be a peer, a teaching assistant or perhaps a youth worker.

Carers who observe their young people acting in a risk-taking way often feel they are 'losing' their children. However, adolescence is a time of transition, and the young person will normally want their parents or carers and siblings in the background and may even wish to have extra discipline, such as stricter time boundaries or rules of the household, such as cleaning duties, to help them. The balance between offering support and giving a young person independence and time on their own or with friends is always delicate one and even more so at this time. However carers and professionals should never give up and just let the young person act in a risky manner, as they will appreciate the repetition of offers of help, a regular meal, offers of having a friend around, and asking if they wish to talk even if they do not show it.

Case study

Edward was a 15-year-old boy who had lost his father in a climbing accident. His father had been a very significant figure in his life, taking him on adventure trips and inspiring him. The accident had happened when his father had been away climbing with a friend, and his family were told as soon as possible after it happened. At first, after the loss, Edward became very introverted and refused to talk or tell anyone what he was feeling. He tried to continue at school and with his friends as if everything was normal, though his family were deeply affected and grieving in various ways. His father had been a very strong figure and feelings were not something he ever discussed. Edward stepped up and tried to be 'the man of the house'.

Edward was offered bereavement counselling at school, but refused this at first. His friends struggled to know how to talk to him and began to leave him on his own, as they had little they could say to him, and no concept of how he was feeling. His schoolwork started to deteriorate.

Eventually something exploded in him, and his personality started to change, and he went out all the time. He stopped attending school regularly, was found in the town centre drinking alcohol and taking other substances on an almost daily basis and mixed with another group. He stopped trying to be the man of the house, stayed out late without telling his family where he was, and finally was found in a stolen car with another boy, and taken into a police station to be formally charged.

The police attended his home and talked with Edward and his family. Seeing the police family liaison officers in his home for the second time in a few months was a turning point for Edward, the first time having been when they were told about his father's death. They spoke to him both alone and with his family.

His family were deeply shocked by this behaviour and its consequences. Edward's mother had not been managing well and had not always recognised the grief that Edward was feeling or had not known what to do. His younger siblings had been the priority and they had thought Edward would get through it. They talked more openly with him about what he needed, and agreed to find a support worker or counsellor for Edward, someone he could talk to or just meet up with, while he waited for the court case. Edward finally realised that he might have to accept support or his future would be ruined – he realised that his father would never have forgiven him for that.

> Edward slowly recognised the very deep grief he was carrying, as he met with someone that his school and the police together chose for him. He knew he could not take back his actions in stealing the car, and would always have that conviction on his record. But he began to use the meetings to work out why he had changed personality and what effect his father's death had actually had on him. School staff also met to discuss how they could have supported him and his family differently, rather than let his behaviour slide to the level it had. They recognised that a bereavement policy might have enabled the staff to support the family sooner, and to identify Edward as a young, vulnerable person in need of ongoing support.
>
> Edward eventually calmed down, recognising what he had done to his life, but that it was not too late. As he was under age when convicted of an offence, he was given a fine and a warning. He attended a group for other young people who had lost their fathers, in a local bereavement charity, and found that he was not the only one to have such feelings of rage, which could lead to the behaviours he had shown. He found this very supportive and it enabled him to finally face his future without his dad. He began to concentrate on school life and having fun again, and his family were more open in their ways of managing life without his father. Although he continued to grieve, he also found time to think about the future and remember the past, hoping that his father would have finally been proud of him.

Over-sophisticated emotional reactions

Just as young people will sometimes choose risk-taking behaviour to express their feelings, so at other times they may choose to try and become over-sophisticated. This could take the form of becoming the parent figure both to siblings and their own parents. It can also include feeling different from, or even superior to, their peers, which then sets them apart from their peer group. Trying to become sophisticated actually means choosing to take on adult roles too soon. It is one of the typical reactions of mid- to older-aged adolescents who experience severe loss, as their reaction is to say to themselves unconsciously that they are going to skip the final part of adolescence. This means jumping the part that involves exploring and discovering their identity and confirming their personality, as well as peer relationships, and moving straight to the adult world of responsibility. These young people tend to take on too much responsibility too quickly, become the carers for others and quite often choose jobs and employment in which they are the carers for others.

One of the main dangers of this over-sophistication, is that the teenager avoids their own grieving process. As adolescents are already in transition and moving towards adulthood, young people who choose the over-sophisticated route are choosing one that avoids the big feelings, usually because they are too painful or there is no time to experience them, or because they simply have no choice. This can be the case if, for example, they are the child of a single parent with no other parent figure, or the elder sibling who already held family responsibilities before the loss. But it can also happen as a result of a personality that is simply unable to process deep grief alongside the changes of normal adolescence.

Suggestions for support

Carers and professionals who try to support such young people can help them to make wise choices and enable them to enjoy at least some of their later adolescence. It is difficult to say to these young people that they should return to adolescence in order to feel pain, as quite naturally they would not wish to do so. But if they understand that by choosing this route they are also choosing to grow up fast, perhaps missing out on the fun and growth that adolescents can have, as well as the exploration of their identity, beliefs and different paths in life, they may consider the possibilities. Saying such things to them as:

> *We notice that you now seem to take on all the jobs of your dad/mum. Have you thought if it is right for you to do all that at your age? There are still some things you could do to be a teenager while you can. We know you miss him/her but it does not mean you have to grow up this fast. Let us know if we can help.*

Schools can say to these young people:

> *You seem very old for your years now, it must be tough now you have lost your [loved one], but don't forget you are still a teenager and you have a future ahead of you. Let us know if you ever want to talk to anyone about your life now.*

Reminding teenagers that they are still young and that, although they may plan for future adulthood, they are not at that stage yet, can help them reflect on the choices they have made. Remember, though, that some of the young people who choose to become over-sophisticated as a result of loss simply have no choice but to do so.

Sleep Issues & Spiritual Responses to Loss

Young people may be affected by their loss and show it solely in their behaviour, either by complex or simple reactions as has been shown above. However, it is also usual for young people and adults to have some sleep issues and other more spiritual concerns, particularly if the loss is from a bereavement.

Sleep issues

Issues with sleep and disturbed sleep patterns are typical for young people and adults who experience all forms of loss. Most bereaved people will be affected by dreams about the lost person, which can be either disturbing or comforting, depending on the nature of the bereavement and the stage of grief they are experiencing. Patterns of sleep can be erratic and young people can find themselves unable to sleep for most of the night due to thoughts, images or strong feelings. If teenagers do have a full night's sleep, this is often not refreshing or nourishing, and they might wake up very tired or irritable. Those experiencing loss are inevitably fatigued, as the emotions of loss are usually felt very physically, often surprisingly so. Young people may have little prior experience of this, and may therefore be disturbed or frightened by their reactions. In addition, feelings hidden during the day can emerge at night, and it is not uncommon for young people to cry alone at night, but not to tell their families or friends.

For those who are disturbed by changing sleep patterns, sometimes just knowing that this is something nearly all bereaved people experience is very helpful. Being bereaved, as well as experiencing loss from other causes, is a very tiring experience, and sleep is necessary. However many bereaved people report that although they sleep for long hours they do not feel refreshed. Therefore young people will need to be reassured that they are not alone if they also feel this, and that things will change as their experience of loss changes. Given that adolescence is a challenging time anyway, during which exams and schoolwork, relationships, emotional changes and hormonal changes occur, a lack of refreshing sleep can be very difficult for young people to manage.

Suggestions for support

Ways to support a young person in having a more refreshing night's sleep can include the use of calming essential oils in a bath or a burner, encouraging them to listen to calming music, reading a good book, or some stress relief techniques such as meditation or yoga (See Resources, 'Further Reading'). If the teenager is not interested in these suggestions, it may be helpful to find out if they have their own ideas.

Having dreams about the one they have lost is also typical for all bereaved people. Reassuring young people that their feelings and responses are normal can be useful. They may also find it helpful to talk about their dreams if they are disturbing and can remember them. Some young people will like to retain their dreams, as this keeps the memory of their loved ones alive. Other young people will find it strange and worrying. Therefore saying such things as:

> *I am really sorry your sleep is affected by your experience of loss. You know it is normal for this to happen, but if you are having particular dreams, do let me know. Sometimes it helps just to talk about them.*

> *Dreaming of [name of loved one] is quite normal, and sometimes it can bring such big feelings, both of loss and remembrance. Let me know if you ever need to be comforted or just to talk about what it is like to dream of someone you love and who is no longer here.*

In addition, it can be helpful to mention the tiredness if the young person seems particularly tired and unrefreshed after sleep:

Because of your recent loss, you will be tired more than usual, as losing someone is a surprisingly physical experience isn't it? You may feel tired for a while, and hopefully your sleep will improve soon. Allow yourself just to rest when you can, and school will give you a time-out card so that you can leave lessons whenever you feel you can't concentrate or stay in class.

We can give you some suggestions to help you sleep better if you like. If not, do you have any of your own suggestions for how you might get a better night's sleep?

If you suspect that the young people are crying or deeply upset at night and not wishing to tell anyone, you can discreetly ask about this:

I wonder if you are sleeping all right at night? People often have disturbed sleep after losing someone special and quite often the night-time is the time when it is hardest to keep it together. Would you tell us if you are upset at night? We really do want to know.

Spiritual Reactions

Spiritual reactions to loss particularly occur for young people when their loss is from bereavement, although other losses, such when a family member goes into military service and therefore faces death, could also cause these. As teenagers are facing the development of their own identity and making sense, therefore, of the world around them, the need to find meaning in their loss is very important. This can lead to very spiritual forms of seeking and questioning about the meaning of life and about aspects perhaps previously not thought of, such as destiny. The search for meaning can be a valid way for young people to manage their losses and make sense of their life experience.

Some young people may already be members of faith communities, usually following in their family's footsteps, but others will be questioning both their own and their family's beliefs. Experiences of loss can trigger a deeper questioning about what death is and where we go afterwards, but they can also prompt thoughts about the existence of God, the purpose of living and associated values. Teenagers may need help at times to explore these concepts. If they were believers in God, they can become very angry that God has taken away someone they loved and can turn away from their faith. Alternatively, if they previously had no faith, they may begin to find they need to believe in God, or in a bigger force than themselves.

When a significant death occurs for a young person, they are forced to face the fact of their own mortality and that at some point everything dies. This can lead to profound soul-searching for some adolescents, as they attempt to make sense of life and their future place in it. Occasionally this spiritual seeking can have unfavourable outcomes, such as suicidal thoughts and questions about the meaning of life in a negative, destructive sense.

Suggestions for support

To help support these spiritual responses to loss it can be useful to offer time to discuss the issues together as a family, or even as a group in school or another venue, facilitated by an adult. Encouraging a young person to share thoughts and feelings about the meanings of their loss is the most helpful form of support. This could then lead to the young person having some guidance for their spiritual responses (see Toolkit, 'Questions about a Bereavement'). Things that may be helpful to say include:

> *It feels very important for you that you can ask questions and begin to understand what happened and why. Remember that we can be here at any time to help you think through these thoughts and questions.*

> *You seem to be questioning everything and trying to make sense of your loss and how [name of loved one] died. This seems really important to you as a way of managing, but remember that if you ever feel you cannot manage, we are here for you.*

> *You have had to face something very young that not many young people have had to face. It isn't easy coming back from that, and I guess you are trying to make sense of it any way you can. The important thing is probably to keep talking, thinking and checking out with someone you trust, either someone in the family, a friend or someone at school. If you don't have anyone you feel you can talk to about this sort of thing, we can arrange for that at school, as you may prefer to talk to someone who is not involved. Just let us know.*

If you suspect that a young person is becoming suicidal or fixated on the idea of meeting with their loved one in another place, which can happen with some who are exploring their spiritual responses, it can be very important to face this directly, saying for example:

> *We know how upset you have been and how much you are questioning life and everything. We just need to know if you are actually thinking about doing something to end your life. It's a difficult question, but it is really important that you answer it honestly; if the answer is 'yes', we will try and find someone for you to talk to as soon as possible. There are ways to help you if you are feeling this.*

Many professionals find this sort of question hard, as they wonder if by mentioning suicide they are actually going to make things worse, but in fact this is never the case. If the young person has been thinking about suicide they will normally say so, but if they have not, they will usually say that they would not do it. If the young person says they are thinking about suicide but would never do it, or just that they want to be with the person who died, this is very different from actually having a plan to take their life.

Case study

Amelia lost her brother Tony when she was just 13 years old. He was an older brother and had had a car accident. She was distraught, as she worshipped him and had always been so proud of him even though they sometimes argued. For quite a few months after his death she had disturbing dreams of him returning to the house to pick up some of his things. She was also very disturbed by visions of him in the ambulance and hospital where he had been taken as he did not die immediately, an experience that had been very upsetting for the family. At first she found these dreams frightening, then comforting, and then she wanted just to be there with him all the time. She looked forward to night-time so she could dream of him again, although she did not dream every night. She looked very tired on most days, and was very quiet much of the time. She would cry herself to sleep, not telling her parents, because they were also devastated. She would then find it very hard to wake up in the mornings, as the reality of her loss would hit her again.

After some months school noted that Amelia was continually looking tired and unkempt, and that she could not concentrate in class. They knew about her brother and asked if there was anything she particularly needed. She had already been given a time-out card and the offer of speaking to someone. She finally wondered if she should tell someone, so she asked to see a teaching assistant she trusted. She then told the assistant what had been happening at night. After meeting with her two or three times, Amelia began to realise that she was exhausted, and perhaps in need of some extra help. The teaching assistant encouraged her to tell her mother and father, as they would want to know what was happening and were probably very worried about her.

Amelia finally told her parents what she felt at night, and they all cried and shared together how hard it had been since her brother had died. They all realised that they had not talked about it, and were trying to protect each other from the pain of loss which they were all experiencing separately. They agreed to do things together and planned for what to do on his birthday and at Christmas as a family, so that they could grieve and remember him together. Amelia's dreams began to fade, which though she was sad about, she knew was right. She still had problems sleeping for another few months and felt quite low at night. But she was able to tell her parents, and slowly together they started a life without her brother.

Conclusions

Adolescents show their loss in many ways and have quite complex reactions to grief and loss. Some reactions are mild, some are severe and most do not need external help. Often, having someone supportive available to talk to, or who can offer extra quiet time (whether peers, family or others), can be enough for most grieving young people. When reactions to loss are complex, or the emotional or behavioural responses show that more is needed, extra support either from a counsellor, art therapist, or other professional can usually help. Families are vital in their support of young people, and even if they do not consciously acknowledge this, most young people would want their families to know how they feel, despite their developmental need to mix with their own age group and move away from the family circle. However, schools and school professionals can be significant in supporting young people at all stages of loss, and in identifying if extra support or some time out is needed.

Chapter 4
Questions & Comments from Adolescents

Why was I forgotten?' Mary said, stamping her foot. 'Why does nobody come?' ... 'Poor little kid!' he said. 'There is nobody left to come.'

It was in that strange and sudden way that Mary found out that she had neither father nor mother left.

(Frances Hodgson Burnett, *The Secret Garden*, 1911)

When there are issues of loss and grief during adolescence, young people may have questions they wish to ask, which need appropriate responses. However, adolescents may not wish to show their needs openly by asking direct questions, as they are in a stage of development in which they are questioning all their previous parameters in life, including the support of adults. This can cause some reluctance on the part of teenagers when asking for direct support. Young people are also developing their own ideas about issues related to life and are forming their own belief systems and identities, which will become more formed as they become adults. They may therefore ask more 'existential' questions, such as about the nature of life itself or questions that have no definite answers and are a search for meaning.

They may also make comments that may or may not lead to a response, but which indicate their queries indirectly. They will often have mixed reactions to the very idea of adults supporting them, and adult guidance can be rejected in favour of peer support. Adolescents can also deny that they need support or can change their behaviours as a way of managing their experience of loss. This chapter covers some possible questions, responses and comments, as well as giving guidance that may be helpful when either offering support or attempting to engage with young people who have experienced loss. These are divided into different categories.

- On death
- On behaviours and responses to loss
- On schoolwork and friends
- On social media and related contacts

Questions & Comments from Adolescents

On Death

Many of young people's questions and comments about death and dying are ones to which there are no clear answers. They are trying to make sense of death itself and the nature of dying. They are also trying to understand their own reactions. Therefore the various responses to the questions below can be related to how they feel, what they may believe has happened, and what others believe. Most of these queries can also be the starting point for a longer discussion if the young person wants this, to help in their grieving process. Remember to ask if they hold a particular belief or are from a specific faith background if you are a professional supporting young people, before mentioning issues related to religion or beliefs about what happens at death and after.

Also included in this section are a few basic questions that may be asked by teenagers who are younger emotionally and who need reassurance around some of the basic questions more often asked by younger children.

What does death mean?

This can be both a very basic question and a very sophisticated question, depending on the age, maturity and background of the young person. If the question is asked by someone who has either regressed due to a severe and unexpected loss, such as sudden or violent death, or who is generally a very young teenager, it is best to answer with the honest:

> *We don't really know what death means, but we do know it means the body has stopped working and the person can no longer breathe, talk, walk, speak, or respond in any way. They can no longer be present in our lives.*

This answer can help a young person begin to make sense of a loss. It can also have the effect of allowing the young person to show feelings that they may not yet have shown, such as anger that the loss has occurred, and sadness at their loss.

If the young person asking the question is older, more mature, or clearly wants a more spiritual or sophisticated answer, it can be helpful to say, for example:

> *It is hard to know what death means, as we can't go there and ask someone. But many people over the centuries have thought about it and wondered if there are places we go to when we die, or if it is simply the end of life.*

If this answer is not enough, or if it becomes a discussion (perhaps one that brings up deep feelings), young people could continue to discuss this with their peers or family. These questions are asked as a basis for the teenager making sense of their own loss from death. This can then lead to comments such as:

> *All life comes to an end at some point, very few things live for ever.*

A further answer could be:

Many people and religions have thought they have the answer to eternal life, but sadly we have not found it yet. It's hard to make sense of death when you aren't ready and are still young, but sometimes, thinking that we all have to die at some time, helps us appreciate the life we have left.

Referring to the particular loss of the young person asking the questions is usually really helpful at this point, as it may be that they have lost a sibling, or an older relative or parent, and each situation will have a different reaction.

Why did they die? Why did they die young?

When young people ask questions like this, they are actually trying to make sense of their loss and asking fundamental questions about life. Therefore, it can be very helpful to reflect some of this in the answers, saying such things as:

It seems very hard to understand why they have died/why they died young. No one really knows when a person is going to die, though we always hope it will be when someone is older. We only know that death happens at the end of life, and sometimes sooner than we hoped.

It is so tough to think of [name of loved one] no longer being here and not to understand why. There really are no answers, but it's all right to feel pain and loss about them dying as that is the grief everyone feels when someone important dies. I guess that could be why you are asking this. If you want to talk about any of it, just let me know.

Can I see the body?

Young people who ask this question are saying they need to see the body, perhaps to begin a process of saying goodbye, which can happen when someone views the body of someone they love who has died. They may also be asking this question as they are not feeling very brave about actually viewing a person who has died, and yet they know that this is what they want to do. They are also asking for reassurance that if they choose to view the body of the person they have lost they will have support to do so.

Most professionals do say that if a young person wants to see the body of someone they love, it can help in their process of grief and in saying goodbye, particularly if they were not there at the death or if the death was sudden and unexpected. It can also help if they had a difficult relationship with the deceased. It can be important, however, to prepare younger adolescents in particular, by describing what they may see and how the body may feel to them. It can also be helpful to warn them that they may have very strong feelings about seeing the body, but that these are normal and all right, and indeed helpful to their grieving process. Saying such things as:

> *It is your choice to see the body or not, but you may find it particularly helpful to see [name of loved one] as a way of beginning to say goodbye.*

> *If you want to see the body, let's just prepare you first for what you may see, so that when you get in the room you can do whatever you need to, and say whatever you need. You know that the body will be cold, don't you, and that it may feel a little weird? But remember that seeing the body of [name of loved one] is really the first step in accepting they are gone.*

> *Would you like to see the body alone or with someone there supporting you? It is really your choice; some people like to spend a little time alone, but others want to be near someone else, usually from their family. Which would you like?*

Can I get involved in the funeral?

Most young people will not have had much experience of funerals, particularly for a close family member. When young people ask this question, they will need reassurance that they can be part of any service for their loved ones. It is quite usual for young people to help shape a service in some way, choosing readings or music and becoming a part of the proceedings. However, they will need some guidance about how they would like to be involved. Saying such things as:

> *Yes, of course you can help with planning for the funeral. Would you like to think about what you can do to help?*

> *It feels really important that you are involved in the funeral as someone very close to [name of loved one]. Do you know what you want to do to help, or should we think about it together? It will be very important that it is right for you, as the funeral is such an important part of saying goodbye to someone.*

I don't know what to believe any more; tell me what you believe.

A young person may ask an adult what they believe, as they are trying both to make sense of their own loss and build up their own belief system, and hearing an adult talk about their own beliefs can be very helpful. It is important to be honest and to say, for example:

> *Well, I personally believe there is no life after death, and that we perhaps go back into dust or the atmosphere.*

> *Well, I believe in heaven, or something similar, and that we meet our loved ones when we also die.*

Support young people by being honest about your beliefs and what you understand is important for young people during a time of loss, so that they can understand what others think, and begin to decide what they believe themselves. If you are unsure what your beliefs are, it is also fine to admit this, so that young people know that not all adults know everything, which of course, at this age, they already believe anyway!

Young people who have this type of query are usually struggling to make sense of their loss and as a consequence are either losing faith, questioning everything, or wanting a form of belief system to help them through their bereavement and grief process. They are asking for guidance, but also showing that their feelings and thoughts are not clear due to their loss. Saying such things as:

> *It seems that right now you are struggling to know what to think or feel, and perhaps think that listening to what we believe can help.*

> *It must feel really hard after your loss, not knowing what to believe any more, or perhaps you never really knew what you believed – but even more so now. I hope that over time you can work out more what feels right for you.*

You could also say:

> *Well, we know as a family that we believe in/don't believe in God, but it is important for you to choose for yourself eventually, as something like this makes us question everything. We will support you whatever you decide, but now is not the best time to decide. We are happy to talk about whatever you need to think or believe, and hope you can find something that makes sense to you.*

How can God do this?

This is a deep cry from the heart, and not really a question that can be answered. It shows the depth of despair and loss when someone who is possibly a believer, possibly not, questions the death of someone important to them. Loss is a very, very difficult experience for many of us, and young people asking this are simply saying they cannot believe a being who is meant to look after the world has allowed their loved one to die. It is virtually impossible to answer this question, but it is possible to say something reflective and empathic, such as:

> *It's just too hard to understand what has happened and how anyone could let this happen. I really feel how hard it is for you to make sense of this.*

This question is really about the unfairness of the loss and can be answered in many ways, but obviously will need to be answered with great sensitivity as it is clearly being asked by a distressed young person. Answers could include such things as:

> *It seems so really unfair that they have gone and you no longer have them near you.*

Sometimes people are very angry with God, if you believe in God, for taking someone so precious away, but I guess we just don't know.

It's so hard to understand why one person stays and one person goes, we don't really know what is behind it, but if you believe in God sometimes that can help you get through it.

Where are they really? What is death?

A young person asking these questions is clearly still making sense of their loss and, as with the previous question, is asking the ultimate questions about what death is and how they can form their beliefs in their distress. They will know deep down that no one can answer this question, but in their grief and denial they are hoping that they can find out and bring their loved one back. All bereaved people have a time when it is impossible to accept that their loved ones are gone forever, and the fact that death is forever takes some time to fully accept. Young people asking where their deceased loved ones are would like to know the answer to the ultimate questions of how to bring them back, to ask them things they did not have time to ask, and to tell them, perhaps, that they love them, and that they are angry that they have gone. It is possible to say such things as:

We know you really want to understand what has happened, and it is hard to bear the fact that [name of loved one] has gone. Making sense of death may help with this, but it is so hard, as death is the one mystery we can never really solve. But we do have all sorts of theories about it, and ways to help manage it when someone you care about dies. Would you like to know about what might help?

It is also possible to answer such questions with:

Perhaps you feel that if you can understand about death, you can understand what happened. That is a really good idea, as it's the hardest thing in the world to understand about death and someone dying. There are many ways to answer these questions, but obviously we don't really know what happens after death. But we can talk about what you might think, what you would like to think has happened, and even what different religions say about death and dying.

Will I join them when I die? I wish I could see them again. What's the point in life anymore?

Young people who ask this type of question are showing signs of yearning. Their wish to remain close to their loved one is typical and normal for grieving people, including young people. However young people are more vulnerable in grief due to their developmental stage, as they are still adapting to the world, forming their own identities and facing their future adulthood.

Losing a significant person, particularly a parent or sibling, can affect their development and reduce their ability to build a strong sense of self. Therefore the yearning is for a simpler time before they had to experience serious loss and think about their own mortality, something they would normally not have to consider when young. For this reason, also, they may begin to question the very meaning of life and wonder if they should try and join the deceased. Normally this is just a fictional wish, brought about by pain and loss, but just occasionally young people do attempt to actually die in order to join their loved ones. It is therefore very important to clarify their thoughts. You could say empathic and reflective things, such as:

> *You would really like to know if you will meet with [name of loved one] when you die. But of course this is a long way off. It is very hard to imagine life without them at the moment, so hoping you will meet them eventually can be a real help.*

> *Sometimes it is hard to find any meaning in life when you lose someone important to you. It isn't unusual to want to see and be with them again, even if just once, and this is so hard for you. But you know, don't you, that it will get easier over time, or that you can talk to anyone whenever you need to?*

> *I can hear you saying how hard it is to lose someone close to you, and that really you wish you were close to them still. I have to ask this, just for peace of mind: you haven't thought of actually doing anything about this, of considering taking your own life? You know I have to ask that, just to check you are safe.*

How am I going to get through this?

Some young people may want to explore what has helped other people get through their losses, and this can include religious or spiritual practices. So it can be helpful to mention these at times, if a young person asks, for example, a question from the heart of despair. Answers can also include reminding them that there are people they can turn to, either in school or at home:

> *It's hard to know what can help. Sometimes when we face a loss such as a close death, people turn to a faith or a religion, or find some comfort in prayer or similar, as these sorts of practices have been used for centuries to help people cope with bereavement. It might be worth you looking at these possibilities.*

> *If you need someone to turn to, your teacher/assistant/friend may be able to help.*

> *When you feel you simply can't cope any more in lessons, remember to use your time-out card or find someone you can talk to.*

At home, carers can say such things as:

> *We will get through this together, just remember to tell me and come to me if you need to talk or cry or you feel angry.*

Let's think together of ways that will help you to cope, such as helping you sleep using relaxation techniques or trying to have some fun even though you are grieving.

The most important point in dealing with these questions and comments is that young people begin to feel supported, are allowed to choose the level of support and questioning they want, begin to form their own beliefs and choices about death and loss and how to manage their feelings, and are encouraged to ask more questions if they feel the need.

On Behaviours & Responses to Loss

Young people's queries and comments about their circumstances and how they feel are significant, as many young people do not have the confidence to speak openly about their emotions or what they would like as regards support. Many would prefer to be private or share only with their peers. The ambivalence that many adolescents have about support and communication with adults, even close adults within their family, makes this aspect of support crucial when comments and questions occur. While young adolescents are still more dependent on their parents and carers, older adolescents will attempt to be independent even at a time of deep loss and grief. The following questions and comments cover some of the issues that young people may raise.

Where am I going to live? What's going to change?

Young people asking this sort of question are clearly worried about how their loss will affect their future. The questions can relate to loss from death or from other causes, such as divorce, separation and other forms of loss. Although very young children ask this question because they are concerned that things stay the same, young people tend to ask this to make sense of their loss and to check if they will have to adjust to yet more change. Adolescents are able to adapt if they have information, but they would prefer not to have changes at all, unless they choose them. Giving reassurance, if possible, and promising to be honest about any changes, can be very helpful at times of loss.

I promise to tell you of any changes and moves that have to happen as a result of our recent loss. It must be very hard not knowing, so keep asking me and I will promise to keep talking to you.

We know you need to know about any changes, especially if you are moving house or school. We can tell you what we know when we know it, and if possible you can help decide what sort of changes are best for you, though it may not be possible to control if we have to move house or choose the school.

Questions & Comments from Adolescents

Why can't I be independent? I am fine, what's the problem? I am not upset or angry so why are you bothering me?

These sorts of questions and comments are very typical of adolescents generally, and if they occur at a time of loss, the young person is saying that they wish to deal with the issues of loss in their own way, if possible. However, it may also mean that they are trying to protect their family from their own problems, and for this reason it can be helpful just to remind young people that, even though they prefer to be independent, there are people to talk to if needed, or even just to share some time with.

> *It's fine to be independent if you want to, but just remember we are here to talk to if you need us. And that as a family we can support each other.*

> *We really understand that you think you are doing fine, and you probably are. Just remember that sometimes it is good to share what you feel with your family or friends, and if you are, that is fine. We will keep asking you if you are all right as you have had a recent loss and this can have an impact even if you don't realise it.*

How do I deal with this sadness?

When a young person asks this, whether of a professional or a family member, it means they are really struggling and asking for guidance. They may have been crying all night alone, or feel they can no longer talk to their friends. They may have only just realised how sad they feel and that they have never felt this way before. Although adolescence is a time of big feelings, sadness related to loss is one of the largest, most difficult emotions a person can ever experience. It can be completely overwhelming for a young person who is already struggling with feelings and hormones. Using some of the activities in the Toolkit may help.

> *It's really tough now, feeling the pain you feel. The best thing is to let it out when you need to, to tell me or someone else if you cannot cope with the normal things like being in class or going out, and just take time to slowly feel less sad. Try not to be on your own when you feel so sad it is unbearable, as your family/school assistant/counsellor would want you to feel support at these times.*

> *Sometimes when someone feels sad, a big cry really helps. We can also help you to remember that though you are feeling sad, life does go on and you can try and find things to enjoy so that your sadness is not there twenty-four hours a day. If there is a particularly bad time of day, let us know and we will try and support you through it.*

What can I do to help?

This question is often asked by young people who want to be helpful and to protect their families from more pain. It is typical for teenagers to like to be helpful at times of need, even though they can also be selfish and consider only themselves at other times. By offering to help, they are telling their family that they want to be a part of the loss together, and that they know they can do things to make it easier, even if not better. They may, however, also be choosing to take on more grown-up responsibilities to avoid their own pain. Sometimes this is appropriate, such as for older teenagers, but sometimes they may need to remember that they are still just teenagers.

> *We would love it if you can help with some chores, such as washing-up or cleaning, but remember you are a young person with your own life, and we also want you to have fun and to tell us if you get upset. These feelings are normal when you have experienced what we have.*

> *Thank you for offering to help. We can decide together what sort of help is best, but do remember you don't have to do everything, and cooking the meals, babysitting, shopping, cleaning and even other things are all possible, but not all of them, all the time! We want you to remember you are a young person as well as a member of our family experiencing loss.*

It's scary; what should I do about it?

Young people who are asking this question are reflecting on their feelings of fear and being honest and reaching out for help, as they are unsure how to manage their emotions. Adolescence is a time of exploration, risk-taking, belief formation and the building of peer relationships. If a loss has caused a teenager to be scared, unsure and insecure, their process of becoming young adults is interrupted. Therefore, providing support and helping them to continue with many aspects of adolescence, while also helping them to manage any scary feelings they have, will be vital. Encouraging a young person to tell you what is scary, how they have managed to cope so far, and what sort of worries they have will be enormously helpful.

> *I am really sorry to hear it feels so scary. Perhaps you would like to tell me/another person what is particularly scary and we can think together what sort of things might help. It does sound like your recent loss has shaken up your world a bit, so if that is the case, let's think of ways to help you feel good about things again.*

> *It can be hard to feel things are scary, and I am very glad you have said something. Could you tell me what you would like to do, as I am sure things have changed since your loss, and sometimes that is difficult even without anything else? It could be that your parents/us/teachers can find ways to help you plan for what is right for you.*

I need time alone, is that OK?

Young people often need time alone, or with friends, and when a serious loss has occurred, whether from death, separation, someone going into prison or another cause, they will need time to make sense of it, and to adjust. Some adolescents need more time alone than others, but if they are choosing to be alone at all times, never speaking to family or friends and hiding away at break times in school, then this need to be alone could be excessive and should be supported. If the need to be alone is simply part of daily life, or an occasional choice not to take part in family rituals such as meals, that is usually all right. It is best to reassure young people that their choices are fine, but that those who care about them will need to know that they are managing during this difficult time. It is also important to remember that quite often when they are physically alone a young person is communicating with others by text or on social media (see below for more on this).

> *It's fine to be alone; we all know how important it is to be alone at times. The most important thing for us as family/school is to know that you are all right, and are not hiding that actually you do not feel all right. Just let us know how you are from time to time, and hopefully you will join in when you can.*

> *We respect your need to be alone as we know how important it is. If we think that you are spending all your time alone, however, we may check with you how you are really feeling, as that can be a sign that things are not going well and you are struggling. We hope that is all right, and we would only do that as we care/would like to check you are all right given your recent losses.*

Why can't I sleep anymore? Why do I get nightmares? Can you help, I feel so tired?

A young person who is complaining of sleep issues and is tired, or who is disturbed by difficult dreams, is in need of extra support. They may just need to be reassured that this is a normal part of grief, as reactions to grief and loss have a surprisingly physical effect. They may need extra support such as counselling or to be able to tell someone they can trust how they feel. If they do talk to someone, however, they need some responses that can be comforting and reassuring so that they can move through their grief and loss.

> *It is normal not to be able to sleep well after the sort of loss you have experienced. I am sorry that you feel so tired, perhaps you just need a few days of taking things slowly, and we can talk to school/home about doing part-time school for a short while. We can get work sent/send work home, or you can go in/come in for part of each day. Eventually things will be a little better, even though you don't think so now.*

> *We will do all we can to help, but sometimes when someone has had a serious loss, tiredness just does stay for a while. If you are disturbed by the dreams, would you like to speak to someone who might help? Or just spend a bit more time at home with your family? You can really comfort each other at this time.*

Questions & Comments from Adolescents

How can I make sure I remember?

This is a really important part of losing someone for a young person, because one of their big fears is that they will forget the person they have lost. Reassuring the adolescent that they will not forget, and that they can also do things to help themselves remember, will be of use. Suggesting exercises from the Toolkit, or looking at photos and remembering family times together can be one of the best responses.

> *It is so very important for you to remember things about your [mother/father/sibling/ grandparent/carer]. We can do some exercises together, or we can simply talk about them and look at photos. Sometimes people like to make a memory book or journal. Let's think about what will help you to be sure you keep your memories alive.*

I find it hard to concentrate; is it because of what happened?

Young people can often find it hard to concentrate after a loss, whatever the cause. It is a normal reaction to grief and loss, and adolescents will need reassurance that this is the case. It is very important to help them find ways to manage by, for instance, giving them a time-out card at school, or allowing them to take some time off school if their concentration is severely impaired. When strong emotions, such as those caused by loss, are experienced, it is quite usual for everyday life to become out of focus, and adolescents are often given a very demanding routine at school, which can be quite challenging to them at this time.

> *Yes, finding it hard to concentrate is absolutely normal when you have a loss. Hopefully knowing that it is a typical reaction can help, but we can also find ways to support you if you would like that. If you are taking exams, or if the work seems particularly hard and you would normally be able to do it, come and tell your teacher/tutor/allocated person and we can try and give you extra time, or less demanding work for a short while.*

> *Because of your recent loss, we want to do all we can to support you and giving you time to manage is one of those ways. If you find it hard to concentrate, we can give you a time-out card to help. You can use this whenever it feels hard to remain in class and do the normal work, or if your strong feelings suddenly come back.*

Why did you separate and why didn't you wait till I left home?

Young people who ask this of their parents are really struggling to understand adult relationships and often want an honest answer. It is usually best to sit down as a family if you can, and talk about what is happening and what will change, as well as to explain what has led to the final decision to separate. Many young people experience separation and divorce and are able to cope with this change with the right level of information and support. However, it is a loss for them, and it is a big change if there appeared to be few or no previous problems in the relationship. Telling them of plans for the future (such as when they will see each parent and who they will be living with if they have not already given a preference) and asking them what they would like themselves, can both very helpful in managing the break-up of a family that had previously seemed close.

> *I know how hard it is for you to accept that your mum and I are separating now, but we do believe it is for the best. We are not able to live together/have grown apart/are just cross with each other all the time/do not love each other anymore, but we will always want what is best for you, and will always love you.*

> *We will tell the teachers what is happening so they can support you at school, because it can be tough to go through some of these changes. Talk to your friends, if one of them has had parents who got divorced, to see how they feel about it all now. We hope it will get easier over time.*

> *We could not wait till you left home, as that would have been dishonest. It is hard to describe what happens when parents know it is the right time to separate, and we did think of you, but we know it is better this way. I hope you can understand more when you are a bit older.*

Do I have to do more chores around the house?

Young people quite naturally need to take an active part in family life, whether or not they have lost someone close to them. An adolescent who is questioning if they need to do more, could either be asking to be more helpful, or rebelling at the burden of doing more as a result of losing someone important. Obviously it can be very hard for an adolescent to adjust to the changes caused, for example, by a mother who is no longer there to cook every day, prepare clothes, or do the shopping. It is also very important that they only do what is acceptable given their other responsibilities at school, and their need to have a social life and remain an adolescent.

If the young person appears to be offering to be more helpful, it is possible to say, for example:

> *You know that as a result of our loss, things will need to change a bit. I wonder if we need to sit down and decide which things you can help with and which things are too much for you. I would be very grateful if you do some things, as we will all need to share burdens and tasks, and it is hard. We need to decide together as a family.*

If, by contrast, the young person is asking if they really need to be more helpful and are not wishing to, it can be useful to say something different, for example:

> *It must seem hard to you that you have to do more now we have lost [name of loved one]. However, as a family we need to work together so we can survive this loss, and it is hard for all of us. Let me know which tasks you are willing to do, and I will tell you which ones we need you to do. But it should not stop you going out and seeing friends, or doing your schoolwork as we know how important it is to you. Let's keep talking about it all.*

Questions & Comments from Adolescents

On Schoolwork & Friends

How can I do my exams with this going on?

It seems very hard for young people to have to face the stress of exams and complicated schoolwork in the midst of the difficult emotions caused by grief and loss. Sometimes it is impossible for them to focus on this aspect of schoolwork, and schools can negotiate with exam boards on occasion, if the timing of the exam is very difficult for a young person, for instance on the day of a funeral or within a week or so of a serious loss. This aspect of young people's needs is difficult, as some would like to carry on, do their exams and forget their loss, and others know they cannot function normally. Most schools will try and negotiate what is best for the particular young person, which may include resitting an exam at a better time, estimating marks if the exam is part of a modular course, or delaying it. Occasionally a letter can be sent to the examining board describing the nature of the difficulty the young person has been or is facing, so that this is taken into account if they do participate in exams and are clearly not functioning well. Many young people who do choose to sit their exams at a difficult time admit later that they simply were not performing very well, so this last option can be very valuable.

> *We know how difficult this time is. If you feel that the exam is something you simply cannot face, or you think you will not be able to concentrate properly and will under-perform, let us see if we can either rearrange it or speak to the examining board about other options. We cannot promise, but occasionally estimates are acceptable; alternatively we could arrange for you to take it at another time.*

> *Whatever happens, we will sit down with you and try and work out what is best for you, as your loss is clearly affecting your work at the moment, which is understandable.*

My mates don't understand. I'm having problems at school as the mates I used to have just don't understand me anymore.

An adolescent who says this is feeling isolated, something most adolescents feel who experience a serious loss such as that of a bereavement. As the time of adolescence is also the time of forging peer relationships, forming beliefs and creating future adult lives, an adolescent who feels alienated from their peers may be susceptible to low self-esteem, confusion of identity and difficulties in making future relationships. They are also prone to bullying, and comments such as these could indicate bullying of some sort. It is helpful that they have some extra support, or that their peers, if at school, are helped to understand the issues associated with loss. Using some of the exercises in the Toolkit can also help. In addition, encouraging a teenager to speak to someone, perhaps a counsellor or other trusted adult, about the loss they are experiencing, can help them to feel supported so that they can be a more 'normal' teenager when with their peers.

It is really tough feeling that your mates don't understand you. Have you tried telling them what it is like for you? Or would you be interested in talking to someone else so that you can at least explore how you feel? It might be helpful. Then you may feel better about being around your mates for the normal things you like to do, like listening to music and going out?

I wonder if it would be helpful if we arranged for your class to have a special time to talk about loss and grief. We don't have to refer to your experience directly, but you will be surprised how many people of your age have experienced some sort of loss, and hopefully that will make you feel less on your own.

Sometimes it can be helpful to meet with others who have experienced a loss similar to yours. Would you be interested in that? We could arrange for others in the school/ agency to meet together to talk about what it is like. There are also internet sites you can go on [if the loss is a bereavement; see examples in Resources, 'Further Reading and Support'].

It is tough feeling your mates don't understand. I just wanted to check that you are not being bullied for having experienced your loss. Bullying can sometimes happen without you realising it, but it is important you tell someone if that is the case, so that the school can stop it and deal with the bullies.

Can I still go out? Can I still have friends around? I need to see friends and go out so don't stop me.

Adolescents will need to be reassured that they can have as normal a life as they wish when coping with a loss. Sometimes this may clash with the needs of the family for extra support, or perhaps doing extra chores around the house, but it is important for young people to feel they can still see their friends and have fun. It is also helpful for the adults close to the adolescents to keep checking that they are actually all right, as going out can sometimes be a way of hiding from what is really happening.

We don't want to stop you seeing your friends, they are very important to you, but sometimes we may ask you to do extra things around the house or just to talk, as we are going through our loss together as a family.

We know how important your friends and going out are, but we need to check from time to time how you are, as we have all experienced a loss, and sharing how it feels together can be helpful, though of course you can use your friends for support as well. Do tell us if you need to speak to someone else if you feel you can't speak to us.

Questions & Comments from Adolescents

Why is it so important to pass exams and do well?

This is, of course, a standard question from adolescents, but at a time of grief or loss, it is especially helpful to remind young people they have a future beyond their loss. Answering this question, either directly or indirectly, can help focus them away from the distress and difficulties of a loss and back to some of the essence of being an adolescent, part of which is to prepare for adulthood. Being reassured that exams and their future are as important as grieving and facing their loss can be helpful when they feel there is no point anymore.

> *Although you have had a difficult time recently due to your loss, you do still have a life ahead of you, and we/the school/teachers always want a young person to do as well as they can. Focusing on your future and doing well at your exams and work can really help you remember that, whatever happens, you do have a future, and by doing well at exams, you can have the future you want.*

> *It may feel at the moment like exams and schoolwork are pointless. That is often what it seems like when a loss happens and the feelings are difficult. But this will hopefully change over time.*

> *If you really feel you don't have the energy or concentration for the important exams/course work at the moment, we can always speak to school/your teacher about how to help this. We can arrange for extra work at another time, or support for an exam. We know it is difficult at the moment, so no one is going to force you to do something you are not capable of, but at the same time, doing your best can often help you to get through this time.*

I don't want to talk to you, my boyfriend/girlfriend is the only one who understands me.

It is typical during adolescence to turn to peers and girlfriends/boyfriends for support at times of need. If a young person has experienced loss or grief and is feeling well supported by their relationship, this is often a suitable and appropriate form of support. However, it is still important for young people to communicate with their family, particularly if the loss is from a bereavement, so encouraging them to talk to the family (if they wish) can be helpful.

> *We are pleased that your girlfriend/boyfriend is helping you at this time. But please don't forget that we are going through this loss together as a family. If you ever need to speak with us, we are here for you.*

> *It sounds like you believe only your girlfriend/boyfriend understands you, but we do want you to know that we also understand, as we are also going through this loss. Talking to others, either those who have been through something similar or your family, can also be helpful, especially if you feel distressed or confused.*

Sometimes we will want to spend some time together just as a family, sharing and thinking about what this loss means for us. We hope you can be part of this, as this loss means a lot to all of us.

Can you ask the teachers to stop bothering me?

Sometimes a young person who is experiencing loss will not want to be disturbed or reminded of it all the time. If teachers and school have been told of the loss and are asking the young person how they are or if they need to talk to someone, especially if they are doing this openly, it can sometimes seem like interference rather than support. These young people are using school as a way to forget and get away from their difficult experience of loss, trying to make their lives as normal as possible. Being reminded of the loss by teachers in the school environment can feel difficult. The best approach is usually to ask the young person discreetly how they would like teachers and other school staff to respond, whether to say something or not, especially in the early days of a loss. Being discreet when talking to such young people can be really helpful, so that they can choose what level of support they would like from school.

We are sorry if you think we are bothering you. I wanted to have this small chat to ask you how you would like us to respond, as we know you have had a difficult time from your loss and we do want to support you. We can just tell the teachers discreetly what has happened, but not to make a big deal out of it, or we can give you a time-out card if needed. But we will only tell the other pupils if you want that.

We just want to remind you that if you ever want to talk to someone who could help, we can arrange that. We can decide today how you want the school to respond; we will not ignore the fact you have experienced a loss, but we can agree to leave you to manage until you ask for more support. We have told teachers of your loss, and also that they are to be discreet and not talk openly to you about it. You can also decide today if you want any pupils to know. This is your choice.

On Social Media & Related Contacts

For young people brought up in the technological revolution, the use of computers, mobile phones and the internet has created a new way of communication that is very different from the past. Almost all teenagers use mobile phones to text, phone and email, as well as laptops and PCs, media systems and Ipads at home and at school. Young people, just like adults, use these daily and will text and email rather than speak face-to-face at times. Social media sites such as Facebook have changed the way we all interact, both with each other and the world, and young people are profoundly affected by this ability to interact globally.

When a young person experiences a significant loss, whether it is from bereavement or another cause, they are almost definitely going to use social media as part of their daily support. They will use mobile phones, tablets or similar to keep in touch and make arrangements with their friends. They may explore internet sites to find out how others manage loss and communicate with strangers, and they can also place comments on social media sites or other websites, if, for example, they lose a close friend or family member from bereavement. The technology allows for instant communication and instant connection around the world. However, occasionally tension begins to arise between a young person's use of social media to manage their loss, and their home and school life.

Schools often have policies about the use of mobile phones, and internet sites will need monitoring at home, so that they are safe for young people to access. In particular, if a young person is seeking others who have experienced something similar, they may be in touch with strangers via websites, who may or may not be genuine. Though most sites, particularly for bereaved youngsters, are monitored and secure, it is always possible that someone is able to pose as a young person and inappropriately befriend, particularly on unmonitored social network sites. There have also been instances of some sites that appear to encourage vulnerable and unhappy teenagers to commit suicide. It is therefore important to monitor this type of site. Some of the points below may help when supporting young people who are daily in contact with others by social media.

I really need my phone on all the time, but they won't let me at school.

It can be seen as very harsh by young people, who use their phones all the time for many different types of contacts, that they are not able to use them at school. However, young people who have experienced loss could be seen as a special case. They can gain a lot of support and reassurance by knowing that they can be in contact with their family at any time, as a young person who has experienced a loss such as a parental or sibling bereavement, will often be afraid for the surviving parent or siblings. They can use their phones for extra support if they feel distressed during the day and their close friends are not nearby; the phones will keep them engaged when otherwise they may feel isolated and different. It can be hard for school staff to accept that such young people can keep their phones on at school and different schools will have different policies for this. It can certainly be helpful and supportive in the early days of a loss, particularly from a difficult bereavement, for a young person to have their phone with them and to use it discreetly, as long as they stick to rules about when they can and cannot use it, such as in lessons.

> *Because we know you have had such a difficult experience of loss, we are willing to allow you to have the phone with you as long as you accept the rule that it is only to be used out of class and lessons, and discreetly. We know that being in contact with parents and friends can be important for you at this time, and we will review this decision in a few weeks to check if you still need it.*

Leave me alone, I am online with my mates. Why don't you understand, I need to send my messages or I will miss out.

Just as meeting with their friends can seem more important than spending time with family after a loss, so online connections also become important. As young people now use their social media daily, even hourly, to keep in touch with each other, it is very important for them to maintain these types of relationships. However, it can also be important to check that they are contacting in an appropriate way, not being bullied or bullying (see below), not sending inappropriate information, and that they still have time to talk to their family and their friends face-to-face if needed.

It can be hard for adults, who often understand less about social media than do young people, to monitor this level of contact. However, as regards loss, the most important issues to remember are that the young person does need to retain contact with their peers, but that it must not stop them talking or engaging in some way with their family. Parents and carers in particular may simply need to remind the young person to spend time with them, perhaps at mealtimes, during an evening in front of the television, or even while sharing a computer game together. Ensuring this form of contact gives the young person the reassurance that when they are ready, they can talk about how they feel or what matters as regards the loss.

> *We know how important it is for you to keep in touch with your mates online. But please do remember that we are all in this loss together, and as a family we will sometimes do things together. We just want you to know you can speak to us whenever you need to. We will also monitor to check that what you are doing online is safe, because it is our job, even though you are older, to keep you safe till you are old enough to look after yourself.*

The only time I am happy is when I'm texting or playing games on my phone, that's all right isn't it? I don't know what I would do if I didn't have my phone/laptop/computer/tablet.

Adolescents can use their contact with social media or games to escape from the pain of experiencing loss, and everyone has the right to do so, especially when that pain appears unbearable. Part of experiencing grief and loss is the stage of being in denial. However, it is also important for young people to know that there are other ways to deal with pain and to cope with their grief and loss when they are ready, and a young person saying this may actually be saying, 'Help me, I don't know what to do!' Giving a young person options can be useful, while reassuring them that if their need is to escape occasionally, that is fine, as everyone does this at times when they experience loss. It can also be important to check the safety of their contacts if they are searching on sites that allow them to meet strangers and communicate, as mentioned earlier.

If you need to be on the phone most of the time, that is fine. But we do want to check that, when you are ready, you can talk to someone about your pain. Needing to feel happy is important, but when someone has experienced the sort of loss you have, there are bound to be other feelings, and we know how hard it is to recognise them. When you are ready, come to us and we will try to either talk with you ourselves, or find someone you can talk to about this.

We know how important your phone/computer/tablet is. We just need to know that you are using them safely. You have experienced a difficult time, and we know that sometimes when people feel unhappy they do things, or they look for ways to manage that are sometimes a bit unsafe. Is it all right for us to check the sites you are on, and can you reassure us that you are just using the internet to make contact with friends and for games/music?

If the young person is not happy with you checking the safety of sites they are using, it will be important to remind them of 'stranger danger', which is as important on the internet as it is in everyday life. It can be very hard, if a teenager wishes to be secretive, to know exactly who they are communicating with, so the best response can often be to continue to offer support and be available to talk whenever they need. If the young person can reassure you that nothing untoward is being encouraged, that is, of course, best. See Resources, 'Further Reading and Support', for examples of safe sites where young people who are bereaved can gain safe support.

Is my music bothering you? I can put it on silent if you like.

Many young people nowadays only listen to music through earphones, so this may not apply very often, though with the advent of docking stations for MP3 players this is changing again. However, it is important to recognise that music is a very significant part of an adolescent's world, and the music they listen to expresses who they are and what they are beginning to believe, as well as helping them identify themselves as part of a particular group of adolescents. Different types of music represent different groups within the adolescent community, and when a young person experiences loss, their music tastes can change just as their experience of life changes. If their music suddenly becomes louder or softer, or changes tone, this is helping them to express something important about how they feel. Music is often an expression of what we feel unconsciously, and this is as true for adolescents as it is for adults. Music can be a significant help in a young person's journey through grief and loss. If they do wish to have their music on loud, it could be because they are changing tastes and wish to show you, or simply because they wish to hear it out loud rather than through earphones.

I wonder what you are listening to at the moment? I know very little about your music, but it seems so important to you and I would like to share that sometimes. If you need to play it loud, just let me know and I will be all right about it. But if you need to be private about it, that is fine too. Music can be very important when we experience loss, and perhaps as a family we can find some music we all relate to at this time and you could help with that.

I hope that the music you listen to you helps you as you experience the feelings we are all experiencing. Loss is a difficult thing and we all choose different ways to manage it. Perhaps music is one of the things helping you at the moment. If that is the case, do let us know whenever you want to share what you are listening to. It may help us all!

Someone is bothering me online; is that cyberbullying?

Just as a young person who has experienced loss and grief is more susceptible to bullying in the classroom or school environment, it is also true that they are more prone to cyberbullying. This is on the increase, as social media and smart phones continue to develop. Young people who are attempting to manage loss are generally more vulnerable and therefore could be more at risk from cyberbullying. This can take the form, for example, of sending inappropriate pictures or videos, emails or texts and placing information on a social media site for all to see. These incidents can be very distressing for everyone.

Young people who experience this form of cyberbullying often do not know how to manage it, or how to respond as their peer group apparently turns against them. Given that young people who are experiencing loss already feel different from their peers, cyberbullying can be a difficult addition to their life experience. If a young person tells you they may be experiencing cyberbullying, it is important to take it seriously and attempt to support them. Many young people do not tell their parents or friends about such bullying, so it can be very important to check from time to time that it is not occurring or that they know how to respond if it is.

There is no single right way to react to cyberbullying, and it does depend how serious it is. However, it can be taken seriously enough to inform the police and instigate official procedures, if it is covered by the 1994 Harassment Act, which includes acts such as persistently sending abusive texts or emails. Most younger schoolchildren are now taught to 'zip it, block it and flag it', as a way of managing any form of cyberbullying. Adolescents need encouragement to do the same. However, a vulnerable young person may need support to manage this, and to respond in an appropriate way. It is possible, if the bullies are known to the young person and at the same school, for the school to take the matter out of the realm of social media and to openly discipline such bullying.

> *I am sorry to hear you may be experiencing cyberbullying. You know we have a zero tolerance attitude to bullying of any form, and cyberbullying can also sometimes be illegal. I am glad you have told someone so we can follow it up and close the site down/ trace the perpetrators. You know that gaining support from your friends, a counsellor, or other trusted adult is one of the best ways to counteract any bullying, as it is simply a form of cowardice.*

Questions & Comments from Adolescents

Is it all right to post a memorial to [name of loved one] online, there's this great site?'

There are many ways for young people to use the internet to remember someone who was important to them, and there are an increasing number of memorial sites which have been set up with this in mind (See Resources, 'Further Reading'). Setting up an online memorial can be a useful way for a young person to begin to adjust to their loss, as the internet and social media are now indispensable for young people to communicate with each other. Often, the first time a young person will tell their friends that their loved one has died is online, rather than face-to-face. In addition, the social media pages of those who are deceased are often kept open so that people who knew them can post messages and photos. Adolescents are particularly knowledgeable about the use of social media internet sites, so their use of such sites can often guide their families and other adults. The main issue, as ever, will be that of safety and appropriate content, which can easily be monitored.

Some families will not wish to have an online memorial site or have pictures posted on the internet of their families. If this is the case, it will be important to discuss with the young person how else to remember their loved one, if the loss is from a bereavement. It will be important for them to understand that not everyone wishes to use the internet to be open about their feelings.

> *It is a great idea to set up a memorial site for [name of loved one]. I would love to know how you do it and to join in, maybe helping decide what goes on. But if you want to do it just for you, that is fine too. We all have our own ways to remember [name of loved one], and this is certainly one way. Please could you just let me know what you put on it and how to access it?*

> *We understand that you want to use the internet to help in your grief. But I feel we need to discuss if that works for all of the family, as putting things like private photos up on site is not for everyone. Can we please discuss this so that everyone is happy with what we do?*

Chapter 5
A Toolkit of Activities

Activities and Exercises

Young people can benefit from activities and exercises that help with various aspects of loss and grief, if used in the right circumstances. In this chapter you will find suggestions that can be used with both individual adolescents and groups: suitability for individual or group use is given at the beginning of each activity. Photocopiable worksheets to accompany the activities are to be found following the exercise that they are designed to support. These practical resources are divided into four sections:

General Activities on Issues Related to Grief & Loss

Activities for Enabling Feelingss
   These are suitable for all feelings, including anger, sadness, confusion, loneliness, happiness, worry, fear, anxiety, intrigue, emotional numbness, surprise, dismay, shock.

Activities for Working with Specific Feelings
   Anger
   Sadness
   Fear & Anxiety
   Happiness
   Insecurity & withdrawal
   Memories
   Relaxation

On Death & Dying

All of the activities are tried and tested ways of supporting young people as they begin to adjust to their losses. Some of the activities can be done over a period of time, such as the journal-making exercises. Some are suited to groups, others are more suited to individuals; this is indicated at the beginning of each exercise.

When undertaking activities related to bereavement and loss, it is important to prepare your sessions carefully and to manage your activities so that the young people involved gain maximum benefit according to their own needs.

A Toolkit of Activities

Guidelines for Using the Activities

Emotional preparation

- Supporting young people in grief and loss can be an emotive exercise, therefore it is very important to acknowledge the emotional reactions you as an adult can have when young people are affected by loss. Those adults who have had a recent bereavement or another severe form of loss are not usually suited to immediate support for young people, though young people often benefit from knowing that adults can manage and survive losses.

- Ensure that you are ready to allow strong feelings and responses to the activities, and that you feel able to be honest and empathic if the young person shows distress. Enabling grief support always causes reactions, and it may remind adults who have had their own losses of these.

- If you are not a trained counsellor, be aware that the skills of listening and reflective response and the art of silence, rather than making the 'right' responses, are all helpful at times of distress. Examples of reflective, empathic responses would be, 'It sounds like you are very sad/angry', or 'I am wondering what that was like', instead of asking direct questions.

- Strong feelings such as anger and sadness can evoke strong reactions in adults. Prepare yourself in advance by acknowledging the way in which these feelings are a normal reaction to grief and loss, and imagine how you might feel if you experienced a similar loss. It can help to reflect on the times when you have had strong emotional reactions to experiences. This will help in your acceptance of feelings such as anger that might be expressed by young people, although of course the normal rules of discipline must always be kept.

- Sharing distressing situations with young people can be distressing in turn for adults; therefore identify when you may need extra support yourself, or when you may need to walk away rather than say something inappropriate or show your own emotions. In a school the conflicts between the role of teacher and the role of supporter, for example, may need to be considered before deciding who offers the support and who is most confident and able to offer this.

Practical preparation

Prepare the room: for example, think about tables, seating arrangements, cushions and resources needed for each structured activity in advance. Remember to keep the environment safe and relaxed, in order to allow young people to show their needs where possible. Young people who experience loss are often feeling defensive and unsure, therefore an environment that is familiar, well-prepared and not anxiety-provoking is important.

Time and place

- Consider the time of day for offering each activity, and choose if possible times when a young person can spend some time after the activities alone, or with friends, rather than returning immediately to a busy school environment. Before break and lunch times, or after school if appropriate, are all suitable times.

- Ensure that there is another adult available after the activities for follow-up support, if needed. This can be important, for example, if a young person becomes emotional or angry in some way, and needs to talk or calm down. A young person who is experiencing loss can also feel very vulnerable after activities and need some time alone, with a supportive person nearby if they need to talk at some point after the exercise.

- Ensure that you have planned enough time for questions, upset feelings and for discussion/reflection, either as a group, or individually. Also ensure that you do not have a pressing engagement immediately after the exercises so you are available for young people who may need extra support or some time out after an exercise.

Seating arrangements

Consider the following when planning each activity:

- How many young people will sit at a table, in a circle or on cushions in a room?
- How many young people you would like in the group, or how many can practically undertake an activity at any one time?
- Who in the group has experienced recent bereavement or loss?
- Where is it best to seat those who are more vulnerable due to recent loss, perhaps close to friends or others with a similar experience?
- Who has difficulty in group situations?
- If offering individual activities to a group of young people, consider who can be near them for extra support and who can sit together while undertaking individual exercises.

Create a relaxing environment

- The more safe young people feel in your environment, the better they will be able to use the exercise and the more helpful this will be for them.
- A room that is pleasant and relaxing will greatly enhance this sense of safety, even for much older teenagers.
- You can aid relaxation by changing some of the rules of dress and uniform, for example: by having everyone sit on cushions, or on a carpet, or by taking off their shoes.

A Toolkit of Activities

- Music can be used to create a relaxed and informative atmosphere, though the choice of music will be significant. Classical music and calming music are obviously more beneficial than loud rock music for relaxation purposes. However, young people may relate more to the music of their own era, and could perhaps be given the opportunity to choose their own pieces of music at certain times. In addition, when feelings such as fear and anger are being explored, music for calmness and relaxation may feel less appropriate, and music which reflects those feelings can be chosen.

Facilitating a group for teenagers

- All teenagers are self-conscious. Therefore any group related to feelings will need to be carefully planned and a facilitator needed to enable them to listen, talk and be honest. This can be helped by putting them at their ease, encouraging them to each take turns, and to listen.

- A facilitator's role is basically that of helping the group members to talk to each other, to keep within the allocated time, and to stay within boundaries by not being rude or physically abusive, for example. Most teachers of young people will be able to do this fairly easily; others may need a bit of extra support.

- When starting a group, remember to create a 'group contract' at the beginning, which all members help create and can agree on. Examples of what can go into this include guidelines for: confidentiality; allowing people speak without interruption, acceptance of feelings; indicating that extra support is needed (e.g., by putting a hand up); keeping to the time boundaries; and for only offering respectful comments to each other about creative work (e.g., no physical violence). See the template in Resources, 'Sample Group Contract for Adolescents' for suggestions as to what might be included.

- The use of a 'talking stick' to be held by the person speaking can allow each young person to say something about themselves and enables taking turns.

- The assumption of this book is that the group will already know each other. If this is not the case, the sessions might be structured differently to allow time for 'ice-breakers' or similar warm-up exercises. The group can also finish with one activity that does not relate to the exercise.

- The facilitator needs to be aware that young people may need to limit what they say in front of each other, particularly if they are not usually part of the same set or group. Encouraging them to take some risks and talk about more revealing aspects of themselves will be enhanced if they feel safe.

- Creating a contract or rules that include such issues as confidentiality is important. Groups can be very supportive, but the best group for young people is one that is secure and safe, has a specific remit, is facilitated by someone they look up to and trust, and in which they are guided to say what they need.

◎ The main skills needed by a facilitator are:

- To be able to listen well and paraphrase what they hear.
- To be able to intervene when needed to help focus the group or to limit or enhance what an individual says.
- To be in the background or take more control when needed.
- To be able to offer reflective comments rather than direct questions, for example, 'It sounds like that makes you feel sad', rather than, 'Does that make you feel sad?'
- To ensure that all group members are able to speak.
- To begin and end the group well.

General Activities on Issues Related to Grief & Loss

Activity 1

The Loss Journal – An Exercise over Five Weeks

Individual ✔   Group ✔

Materials

- A notebook for each young person
- Pens, pencils and art materials, if needed
- Worksheets 1–5 for each person

Aims and Overview

- To make time to reflect on, record and explore feelings quietly and privately; to write down memories.
- The exercise is for all young people, whether or not they have had a significant loss in their life. It is, however, particularly suited to those who have experienced grief or loss at some point.
- The young people are directed to write or draw in their journals some of the feelings and memories that occur during a five-week period. This can be a daily or weekly journal; the group facilitator can provide suggestions about what they may wish to write. They can choose to continue on their own if they wish. They are each given a copies of Worksheets 1–5.

Preparation

Ensure the room is laid out so that young people who wish to write privately can do so and others who wish to sit in a group can also do this.

- There really is no right or wrong way to write a loss journal. Young people can simply use it to 'get their thoughts together', either at times of distress or in anticipation of some of their life experiences.
- Can be undertaken with a whole class, a smaller group of individuals, or just one adolescent.

- Most helpful for young people who are quiet, who are feeling more withdrawn, or who have had difficulty expressing themselves and asking for support. Teenagers who do not enjoy writing could be encouraged to use just a few words and perhaps some other ways of expressing how they feel and what they think, such as simple drawings.

- Ensure that those who need to write quietly can do so, and those who prefer to write and talk can do this without disturbing others.

- Storage of the journals between weeks: if the young people do not wish to keep them at the end of the sessions, a safe, private place must be found. If they do wish to keep them, then the teenagers become responsible for keeping them safe and returning with them for each session.

Instructions

- Prepare all the teenagers by telling them that they are going to write about their feelings and their life experiences, and that there is no right or wrong way to do this. In this exercise all the normal rules (even of grammar) do not matter, as these would inhibit a private reflection.

- Remind everyone that what they write is as private as they want it to be, as no one will be asking them to share anything they have written if they do not wish to. However, after the writing, you can ask for volunteers who do wish to share something of what they have written.

- Remind the group that losses cause big feelings and thoughts, and that it is their choice what they write and what they wish to share, but that writing can often be helpful.

- For those who have not had a significant loss (if this is a whole class exercise), it might be possible, for example, to ask if they can imagine what a bereaved person would write about their loss. Alternatively they could read and write about a character in *Rory's Story* (Jacobs, 2014).

- Give the young people twenty minutes to write in each session. Remind them that they are going to do this for five sessions, but that after the five they can choose to continue with their journal if they wish. The book will become theirs to keep.

- Ask them to choose if they would like to take their journal home each week. If they choose to do so, they must commit to bringing it back for each of the five journal sessions, keeping it safe between times. They can then add to it on their own if they wish.

Discussion

After writing, you can lead a discussion for those who wish to share what they write, examining:

- If others felt similarly while reflecting on their feelings and thoughts.
- If they are surprised by the writing.
- If it prompts them to write more about their own experience.
- If it has helped them to hear of others' experiences.

Activity 1 – Week 1

Worksheet 1

The Loss Journal, Week 1
Introduction to Journal Writing

Write your name on the front page, then the title 'My Loss Journal' and today's date.

Before you start writing, think about keeping a journal:

- Have you ever kept a diary? Or a note of some of the things that have happened to you, either good or bad? Many people of all ages keep diaries and journals to reflect on things that happen to them. This loss journal could help you.

- You are going to be asked each week to write or draw about a different topic. You can write whole sentences, words, a story, poems, draw stick people, or larger drawings. It will be your journal on the different topics.

- If you choose to keep the journal between weeks, you can add to it at home or at school. Try and keep it safe and if for any reason you cannot, tell a teacher who will keep it safe for you.

- To begin this journal today, write 'Part One'.

- What thoughts do you have about loss? Write down some words or drawings about loss.

- Think of a loss, either one you have experienced or one you imagine. Think about how it feels to lose something, and what you would want to do or say. Make up a poem, or write a few sentences, or a drawing.

Page 1 of 2

Worksheet 1: The Loss Journal – Week 1

◎ Next decide if your loss journal is dedicated to someone? Who or what have you lost? Have you ever had a significant loss? If you have not had a recent loss, think of one you have heard about or imagine one. Tell the journal what it is you are thinking or beginning to face and what has happened. Tell it like a story.

◎ Remember to tell someone, a friend, a teacher or other, if you get upset at any time.

Activity 1 – Week 2

Worksheet 2
The Loss Journal, Week 2
Feelings

- Think more about your loss and what you wrote last time, and describe any feelings that you can think of connected with loss. They can be feelings you have had, or feelings that you can imagine anyone having. Write them down.

- Think about feelings like sadness, anger, fear, loneliness, confusion, and so on. Are any of these ones you have thought about? What other feelings are there?

- Have you seen any films or soaps on the television when people are feeling upset about their losses? Think about what they showed.

- Write down as many feeling words as you can. Then try to create a poem, short story, image or drawing, using the words or how they make you feel. You can put the actual words in a shape like a spiral or a square or circle, or you can repeat them on the page. Decide how you want to write these feeling words down.

- Your teacher will tell you when it is time to stop.

- Do you want to share anything you have written? You can choose to do this either in the group, or to someone else you trust.

Activity 1 – Week 3

Worksheet 3

The Loss Journal, Week 3
Memories

- Look at what you have written so far.

- Do any of the words, images or what you have written before remind you of anything?

- Do you have particular memories, either to do with a loss you have experienced, or to do with the words and images you have already written?

- Write down one or two significant memories that are important to you.

- If you have not had a loss recently, write down a memory of something that was important to you.

- Try to imagine a world where we have no memories – if the world was like that, what memories would you be upset to lose?

- Remember you can use words, sentences, poems, images and use repetition or word art (which is when you make shapes out of words).

- Your teacher will tell you when it is time to stop.

- Do you want to tell anyone some of the things you have written? Either your group, a friend, a teacher or someone else you trust.

Activity 1 – Week 4

Worksheet 4

The Loss Journal, Week 4
Things that Have Changed

- Do you feel differently about your loss than the way you felt when you first started this journal?

- Are you able to think about other things, like your everyday life, friends, schoolwork and hobbies?

- If you have had a loss, what did you used to enjoy that you can still enjoy, and what things have changed? Write down any changes you can think of that happen as a result of loss, either generally or to do with your particular loss.

- Do you have a particular memory of change that you find it hard to focus on? What would help that memory?

- Remember you can write words, sentences, a story, a drawing, word art or just repeat one word.

- Is there anything you have written you would like to share? As it is week four, is there anything you want to tell the teacher about journal writing that you do or don't like?

Activity 1 – Week 5

Worksheet 5

The Loss Journal, Week 5
The Future

- As this is the last week of this part of your journal, look back on what you have written.

- Does anything surprise you? What has changed and what is the same about how you feel and what you remember?

- Write about how you feel now.

- Write about anything important that you plan for the future.

- Decide whether or not you would like to keep on writing in this journal, and if you want to keep it or hand it in. Remember that it is private unless you want your teacher/parent/counsellor to look after it.

- Is there anything you want to share that you have written, either today or from the previous weeks? Try and think of one thing you can share, if you can, as sharing something can be very healing when someone has experienced a significant loss.

- Remember to choose if you wish to keep the journal and, if so, where you will keep it. It is yours now and you can add to it whenever you wish.

Activity 2

The Space Story

Individual ✔   Group ✔

> **Materials**
>
> ◎ Paper for each young person
> ◎ Pens, pencils and art materials, if needed
> ◎ Whiteboard and markers
> ◎ Worksheet 6, 'The Space Story', for each person

Aims and Overview

◎ A story-making exercise designed to allow young people to explore feelings of alienation and loss without the story being a direct reference to their own individual experience. This exercise is a safe way for young people to begin to face the feelings associated with loss.

◎ The use of the imagination reduces the vulnerability that adolescents feel when admitting to emotions and responses to loss and allows them to explore the possibilities at a difficult time.

◎ The story is of a spaceman or woman who experiences a new environment, as well as the alienation and homesickness that could be associated with this.

◎ The focus of the story is on how the space person feels and manages this sense of difference, but young people may want to use the story to explore other issues and themes, such as how to make friends, how to communicate, how to fit in with a group, and how they feel about home. All issues very relevant to adolescents.

◎ It is important to ensure that, to begin with, the main themes of the young people's stories are of feeling different, being in a new place, and thinking of their home planet.

◎ Feelings related to this story can include feeling alone, perhaps excited, feeling different or isolated and at times confused by the new things around.

Preparation

Ensure the room is laid out so that young people who wish to write privately can do so, and others who wish to sit in a group can also do this.

Instructions

- Describe the task as creating a story about a lost spaceman/woman who lands on the earth. This can be started with a discussion, for example, on space travel, or thoughts about what is in space.
- Introduce the story-making as an exercise exploring how it feels to be different, in a new place, and to think of the home planet.
- Each group of young people will need a different introduction, depending on their age and experience.
- Encourage the young people to use their imaginations and give each person Worksheet 6 to help them create the story. You could also write the worksheet questions on the board.

Discussion

When the group have written their stories, which may take from twenty minutes to half an hour, ask for volunteers to read their stories out. Are there common themes in all the stories? Are there big differences? Facilitate a discussion to examine how everyone imagined the space person feeling and responding.

Activity 2

Worksheet 6

The Space Story

- Write a story about a spaceman or woman who lands on the earth and cannot get home.
- If it is hard to start, start with the traditional 'Once upon a time'.
- Try and pretend you are the spaceman or woman to see how it feels.
- You can write as the spaceman or woman if you want to.
- What is the spaceman/woman's name and where do they come from?
- Why are they on the earth?
- What do they feel about being on a strange planet?
- What do they want?
- How do they feel different from people on earth?
- How do they manage this 'being different'?
- Do they want to go back home? If yes, why? If no, why?
- Are they alone or have they come with others?
- How can they get what they need?
- Do they communicate with earth people?
- Do they communicate with people back on their home planet?
- What do they do to try and survive on earth?
- Does this story have an ending? If so, what is it? Happy or sad?

Activity 3

Discussion about Bullying

Individual ☒ *Group* ☑

Materials

- Whiteboard and markers
- Worksheet 7, 'What do You Think of Bullying?', for each young person

Aims and Overview

- Bullying can be one of the issues that occur as a result of a young person experiencing loss.
- Loss can be from a bereavement or from other causes such as divorce, moving away, or even an adult in the home who goes to prison.
- This exercise asks young people to consider the impact of loss in relation to bullying. It is a discussion exercise and will need careful facilitation to allow everyone to express their point of view.
- Make sure you know of any particular pupil who has been bereaved of a father, or has suffered severe bullying in the past. If this is the case, allow them to choose if they want to undertake this exercise.
- Place vulnerable young people with friends or other supportive pupils, or a teaching assistant, so that extra support is available if needed.
- See Resources, 'Information on Anti-Bullying Policies' for more information.

Preparation

Ensure that everyone feels safe and comfortable; they could take off their shoes and sit on cushions on the floor if this helps.

Instructions

- Give each young person Worksheet 7, which includes a copy of the little story about John. Allow them a few minutes to read it before asking for responses.

- Ensure that everyone knows that they can express their ideas in the discussion and that everyone must listen to each other. Encourage discussion and allow for time to cover each point raised.

- If you prefer, you can give each of the young people in the group a few minutes to say what they think, in turn, before facilitating a free discussion. Some will have more to say than others

- Make sure everyone has time to say what they think, while guiding them in the following points, which can be written on the board or read out:
    - Bullying is always wrong.
    - Young people have to tell someone whenever bullying happens.
    - Schools can help by having a zero-tolerance policy.
    - Friends can monitor how their peers are reacting if they know of a bereavement or other loss.
    - By gaining confidence in what to say and how to react, young people can support their friends if they know of a loss that has happened.

Activity 3

Worksheet 7

What do You Think of Bullying?

This activity will challenge you to think about how a person who experiences loss may be more prone to being bullied.

Scenario

John, aged 13, returns to school after the loss of his father. He appears fine for the first few weeks, then he seems to be quiet in all of his lessons. He is found in a toilet, looking dishevelled and with torn clothes, and trying hard not to cry. A teacher asks him what has happened but he cannot say. The teacher hopes that it is something that will not happen again. John used to have good friends, but now they do not know how to speak to him, so he has been on his own more than usual. When the same thing happens again, a teacher spends longer talking with John and finally discovers what has happened. The class bully had decided to pick on him as an easy target and had pinched his lunch for a few days and is starting to push him around. When he was found in the toilet, John did not want to tell anyone for fear of being picked on even more.

Points for Discussion

- Do you know what John may be feeling having lost his father? Think about what it might feel like to lose a dad.

- Think about your mates – how would you feel if they were being bullied?

- Consider what level of bullying it would take to get you to hide in the toilets at break time?

- If you were a friend of John's, would you have abandoned him like his friends seem to have done?

- What do you think of bullying?

- Have you ever been bullied?

- What do you think John needs now?

- What do you think John needs from his friends, his school and his family?

- How do you imagine the school might stop this sort of bullying happening to other young people?

- Is there a school policy in your school on bullying? Do you know what is in it?

- Now, can you make some decisions as a group? How would you support your mates if this happened to them? What does the school need to do to help stop bullying? What do you need to do?

- If you have ever bullied someone, do you know how it feels to be on the receiving end? Why did you bully? Did you know it was wrong?

- Make a group/class agreement on how to treat bullying and the bullies. Discuss what the whole school policy should be.

Activities for Enabling Feelings

Many emotions can arise as a result of young people experiencing grief and loss. These can include feeling angry, sad, confused, lonely, happy, guilty, worried, frightened, anxious, intrigued, numb, surprised, appalled and shocked. As adolescents are becoming more sophisticated in their range of reactions, so their need to allow these feelings some expression can become more important. This series of exercises are suitable for examining most feelings that emerge, in order to support young people with their reactions.

- Ensure that any young person you are working with feels safe enough to reveal their deeper feelings, and give them permission not to do any of the exercises if they choose. See the notes on preparation at the beginning of this chapter and consider the best ways your group or individuals can feel safe, such as creating a more relaxed atmosphere, using the correct room, playing appropriate music. In particular, if you are working with a group, discuss the ground rules of accepting what everyone says, not interrupting or being rude, refusing to accept bullying, and listening when someone is talking (see Resources, 'Sample Group Contract for Adolescents').

- If the exercise is undertaken as a group, check in advance if anyone has had a recent experience of loss or bereavement, and how they are managing this loss, as this can make them more vulnerable and expose them to negative peer influences, such as bullying and self-exposure, which can lead to low self-esteem.

- Prepare all the young people in advance by talking of the normal feelings associated with loss and grief. Most young people will have felt anger or sadness at some point in their lives, so they should all have a reference point, even if it is simply feeling this while watching a film or a TV programme or reading a book.

- Remember that at this stage of development, peer pressure is very strong. Your task is to help the group to understand that feelings are normal and that showing feelings is acceptable within limits. The limits include, for example, not displaying violent anger that leads to destruction of property or violence towards others. Your facilitation style will therefore be a key element of any exercise. (See the beginning of this chapter for notes on facilitation.)

- Give all young people permission to choose what to share and when. The more they feel in charge of their own feelings and when to expose them, the safer they will be about exploring them within the context of a small group or classroom.

- Emotional literacy is just as important for young people as it is for younger children. If anything it is more important, as teenagers are beginning to explore the world of intimate relations and sexuality. Therefore if these exercises lead to further discussions or queries related to feelings in other aspects of their lives, this can be a positive emotional learning experience.

Activity 4

A Collage of Feelings

Individual ✔   *Group* ✔

Materials

- Large piece of stiff card for each person
- Paper and scissors for each person
- Glue and glue brush for each person
- Magazines, postcards, scraps of material, other craft materials
- Paint and paint brushes
- Felt-tip pens

Aims and Overview

- This exercise is useful for those feelings that remain hidden, for instance, unexpressed anger or sadness, or anxieties and fears. It can be used for feelings generally, or to focus on one specific feeling related to loss. Decide in advance whether it will be used to explore a specific feeling or groups of feelings.

- Collage materials are used to make an image that expresses the feelings of loss young people experience. By cutting and sticking and using different materials, a collage can be a very satisfying way to begin to express all sorts of feelings.

- Encourage the teenagers to experiment with different forms and shapes, as feelings can be portrayed in many ways.

Preparation

- Ensure the room is suitable for art activities, either by protecting furniture or using an art room where it is possible to create artwork safely.

- Provide each young person with a piece of card to use as a base for their collage, paper, scissors, glue and a glue brush.

- Allow up to an hour for the collage-making and sharing afterwards.

Activity 4: A Collage of Feelings

Instructions

Describe the exercise using the instructions below:

- You are going to make a collage of feelings related to loss. Today it will be a collage about [give the name of the emotion/s].

- Look at the materials on display and think what you may like to put on your paper to display this/these emotion/s. Think for a moment about what it feels like to feel loss. You may have had a recent experience of this, or you may have to use your imagination. If you have read *Rory's Story*, imagine how Rory would display one or more of his emotions.

- When you are ready, gather together some materials and begin to create your collage. There is no wrong or right way to make a collage. It is simply a piece of artwork that puts together different materials and can include drawing and painting, as well as shapes and pictures stuck on your card, all of which will become one piece of art.

- If you have any questions, ask them, and if you have any other concerns, you can also tell me or someone else on your table. But do not interfere with someone else's collage-making. Each of you will have your own ideas of how to do this.

Discussion

- When they have completed their work, they can decide if it truly expresses the feeling they have been asked to explore. If not, why not? If it does, do they know why?

- If they began this exercise full of the feeling, have they changed at the end of the exercise? Has it been a good way to express this feeling for them?

- If group members would like to, they can tell the group what it is they have created. But they do not have to.

- The group leader could also encourage a group discussion about what it is like to have feelings to do with loss, and how art can sometimes help us to express them.

Activity 5

The Scale of Feelings

Individual ✔   *Group* ✔

> **Materials**
>
> ◎ Pens and/or pencils
>
> ◎ Whiteboard and markers
>
> ◎ Worksheets 8, 'The Scale of Feelings', and 9, 'The Scale of Feelings: Discussion and Reflection', for each young person

Aims and Overview

◎ This exercise will help young people to reflect on the strength of feelings without any further expression of those feelings. It enables them to reflect internally on them, before reaching a different stage of seeking help if needed, expressing them or telling someone if the feelings are overwhelming. It is possible for individual young people to do this exercise one-to-one with an adult helper.

◎ If used with young people who are already deeply affected by a loss, it can be used alongside another exercise within this Toolkit related to those feelings, to help them begin the process of expressing and gaining support for deep loss. All adolescents, however, can be helped to become more self-aware as regards difficult emotions, and this exercise enables that awareness.

Preparation

◎ Ensure the atmosphere of the room is relaxed and feels safe enough for young people to begin to consider their feelings.

◎ Provide each young person with the two worksheets, one after another. Allow twenty minutes for completing Worksheet 8, and up to half an hour or more for the discussion based on Worksheet 9.

Instructions

- In this exercise young people are asked to rate themselves for their feelings using Worksheet 8. They will choose four feelings. These can include feelings of despair and sadness, anger, fear, confusion, numbness, anxiety or another emotion. It is a format designed to help them reflect on their feelings without going to the next stage of exploring and expressing them.

- Introduce the exercise by mentioning that it is related to feelings and reactions to loss and grief. It is an exercise during which they are asked to simply think about whether they know themselves and how they feel. The exercise will not be asking them to explore the feeling any further than simply giving it a number on a scale. (There are other exercises in the Toolkit that can be used if their rating indicates it would be helpful to work with one or more particularly strong emotions.)

- Remind the group that they can talk to a teacher, trusted adult or friend for extra support if their responses show a feeling is rated higher or lower than expected, however, they do not have to tell anyone how they feel if they do not wish to do so. Make sure that anyone who has rated feelings at the high end of the scale has the opportunity to discuss this and how it affects them, if they wish.

Write the following prompts on the board to help them:

- Read Worksheet 8 and think about what feelings you can rate.
- Try to find four feelings to rate.
- Remember that if you get upset at any point you can ask for a teacher to help you.
- Your teacher or group leader will tell you when it is time to stop.

Discussion

After they have completed the rating of their feelings, facilitate a discussion regarding their responses, using the previous guidelines on facilitation skills at the beginning of this chapter and Worksheet 9. Write the following prompts on the board:

- Now look at Worksheet 9 and read all the points listed.
- Think about your answers or thoughts after doing the first worksheet.
- Your teacher or group leader will help you to discuss these points in the group.
- Finish by thinking of anything that has helped you understand your feelings better.

You could encourage the group to begin the discussion by asking for a show of hands in response to the first three points on the worksheet.

Activity 5

Worksheet 8

The Scale of Feelings

- Think about an experience of loss you have had, either recently or in the past.

- Now choose three or four feelings that you experienced as a result of this loss.

- Write the name of each feeling in the blank spaces below and rate the strength of this feeling on the scale of 1 to 10, where 1 is 'very weak' and 10 is 'very strong'.

- Circle the number that most reflects how you feel when you think about your loss.

- If you feel upset at any time during the exercise, tell someone, a teacher or another adult.

Feeling One _____

Very weak feelings   Very strong feelings

1   2   3   4   5   6   7   8   9   10

Feeling Two _____

Very weak feelings   Very strong feelings

1   2   3   4   5   6   7   8   9   10

Feeling Three _____

Very weak feelings   Very strong feelings

1   2   3   4   5   6   7   8   9   10

Feeling Four _____

Very weak feelings   Very strong feelings

1   2   3   4   5   6   7   8   9   10

This page may be photocopied for instructional use only. *Supporting Teenagers through Grief and Loss* © Anna Jacobs 2013

Activity 5

Worksheet 9

The Scale of Feelings: Discussion & Reflection

- Who was surprised by their results?

- Who rated their feelings at the low end of the scale?

- Who rated their feelings at the high end of the scale?

- Have you told anyone about this? Do you feel you need to?

- Are you pleased you have rated your feelings higher or lower than expected?

- Sometimes it is helpful to give these feelings a scale, to help others know how deeply you feel, or even so that you can understand how you feel yourself.

- Sometimes it can help to recognise how you feel and to check over a period of time if this changes.

- Sometimes deep feelings come and go, especially in the early days of a loss, and these feelings are not unusual, although they can be hard to understand and cope with.

- Those who do not have experiences of loss can also feel strong feelings at times and it is usually helpful to tell someone if these feelings are regularly at the high end of the scale.

- These feelings can affect aspects of your life, such as schoolwork or being with friends.

- If this is the case, knowing the strength of your feelings can help when, and if, you wish to tell someone this. There is always support available for anyone who experiences feelings related to loss.

Activity 6

Music & Emotions

Individual ☒   Group ✔

> **Materials**
>
> ◎ Music provided by young people and teacher/group leader
> ◎ Pens and/or pencils
> ◎ Whiteboard and markers
> ◎ Worksheet 10, 'Music & Emotions', for each person

Aims & Overview

◎ Young people often spend a large part of their life listening to and enjoying music, including dancing to it, but they may not always recognise the feelings behind the music. Through listening to music in this activity, they will begin to recognise how to use music as a support mechanism. Music can express many emotions and is often one of the main forms of expression for young people. Music can reflect different emotions for different people, and some of the pieces one person may choose as being sad, for example, may not seem sad to other people.

◎ In this exercise you will ask the young people to select some pieces of music that reflect their feelings, and you are going to select some of your own choices too. Then, as a group, you will simply experience the music and respond.

Preparation

Prepare the room in advance. Use a room in which the young people can relax fully, for example lying on cushions on the floor, or with space to spread out. Make sure you have the facilities to play music in this room and that you will not disturb others nearby, as you may want to change the volume from loud to quiet at different times.

◎ The week before the activity ask members of your group/class to try and find a piece of music, something that they like, which for them reflects strong feelings. Ask them to bring it in the following week for a musical experience.

- If possible, ask them to bring it in a form that can be listened to by the group. If they cannot do this, ask them for the details so you can create a playlist in advance on your computer or MP3 player.

- Choose your own selection in advance also. See Resources, 'Music, Poetry and Art Resources' for suggestions of music to use for certain feelings. Choose how many pieces you can listen to in one session, depending on the time you have available. Choose no more than eight and shorten the pieces if necessary. Remember to provide a range of music that reflects happiness as well as sadness, anger, fear or other feelings.

- It may be possible to repeat this exercise more than once if more young people want to bring their selections in.

Instructions and Discussion

Provide each young person with Worksheet 10. After listening to the music and using the table on the worksheet to rate the emotions the pieces aroused, facilitate a discussion based on the points in the second part of the worksheet. They could also think about the following questions if there is time:

- What might it feel like to listen to music alone?
- Would they prefer to listen with a friend or group of friends?
- Did lying down and relaxing made a difference to listening to the music?
- Have they ever used music to help with particular feelings they have had and, if so, which ones?
- How do they use music? For example, during the day when not at school, in the gym, walking or running, dancing to or in the bedroom alone.
- Can they imagine a world without music?
- As you talk, try and listen to snippets of the pieces of music that have been brought in but not played yet. Make sure you put some of your choices on for them to listen to and ask them about their responses.

Finish your discussion by checking if they have found the exercise enjoyable.

Activity 6

Worksheet 10

Music & Emotions

- Find a place in the room to sit or lie where you will feel comfortable listening to music.

- You can sit near your friends or be on your own.

- When the music is on, relax and listen, letting the music flow over you.

- When the music stops, look at the table of emotions below and see which feeling is the one that is closest to the one you felt.

- Put a tick in the first box next to the name of the emotion.

- For the second piece of music do the same.

- After four or five pieces, your teacher or group leader will stop the music.

- Look at your worksheet and compare it with the person next to you.

- Are the feelings that you have ticked the same as your neighbour's?

Page 1 of 2

Worksheet 10: Music & Emotions

	1	2	3	4	5	6	7	8
Happy								
Sad/despairing								
Angry								
Frightened/scared								
Confused								
Anxious/worried								
Numb								
Unsure								
Other?								

Points to think about and discuss

After you have listened to the music, think about your own answers to the questions below. Your teacher or group leader will help the group share their answers.

- How did you feel listening to the music?

- Did you have favourite pieces of music? And least favourite? Why?

- Did any of the music evoke strong feelings or memories? If so, what were they, and are you willing to share these?

- Did any music evoke no feelings? How did it feel to not respond? Was it because you did not like the music?

- Can you think of a time when you used music to help with how you felt?

Activity 7

The Island

Individual ☒   Group ✔

Materials

- A3 or A2 card and scissors for each person
- Paints, brushes and palettes for each person
- Glue and brushes for each person
- White and coloured paper
- Light tissue paper
- Felt-tip pens and glitter glue
- Bowls of different craft items chosen for texture, such as sand, pieces of pasta or rice
- Whiteboard and markers

Aims and Overview

- The young people are going to create an island using art materials. This will allow them to reflect on feelings of isolation and loneliness, as symbolised by the island.

- This is not a verbal exercise, so it can allow a young person the safety of exploring their emotions using art, without the need to talk if they prefer. However, it is always important to offer them opportunity to talk to someone if they feel they need support at any time. An opportunity for a class/group discussion can be offered at the end also.

Preparation

Ensure that the room you are in is suitable for artwork, preferably an art studio or one in which there is a sink and space for each young person to make their own work of art. Also ensure that the atmosphere is one of relaxation and safety, to enable young people to begin to consider the themes within the activity.

Activity 7: The Island

- Provide each young person with at least one piece of large card, scissors, paints, paintbrushes and palette, as well as glue and glue brushes.
- Describe the exercise as below. Allow up to an hour for making the island and sharing afterwards.

Instructions

- Imagine an island on which only one person lives. It can be as sophisticated or as simple as you like.
- Be as imaginative as you want to be, and think of which animals and plants are on this island.
- What size is it?
- How close is it to any other island?
- Is it a friendly place or an unfriendly and dangerous island?
- Is it an island with a history, or is it a new island not yet discovered?
- And finally, on this island, where does this one person live? What sort of home do they have?
- Have they lived there for a long time or have they only just arrived; if so, how did they arrive?
- When you are ready, create your island on the card using the materials available. It does not have to be a big work of art, but try and make something that represents your island.
- There is no right or wrong in this artwork: you can choose the colours, the size, and what is on your island. Try and experiment with the materials.
- If you have any questions, ask them, and if you have any other concerns, you can also tell me or someone else on your table. But do not interfere in someone else's island-making exercise. Each of you will have your own ideas of how to do this.

Discussion

After they have spent up to half an hour creating their islands, ask them to stop and look at their artwork. They do not have to share anything they have done with anyone else. However, you are going to ask them to reflect on their island and how they feel about it. If you ask them the following questions, this will help to generate a whole group discussion:

- Where would you place yourselves on this island?

- If you were on this island, how would you feel?

- Would you want to leave, or stay? Would you want others to join you, or would you be happy to remain alone?

- Does the idea of living on an island appeal to you, or it is a horrifying idea?

- If you were on the island, what would you miss about your present lives?

- Finally, have you learnt anything new about yourselves, such as the fact that you actually quite like the idea of an island, or that you would miss your family too much? Perhaps some things you may not have realised before?

Some of the islands can be left on display for a short time, with the agreement of the young people, so that they can continue to reflect on them.

Activities for Working with Specific Feelings

Anger

Anger is a typical emotion felt by all those who experience grief and loss. It is also, however, a feeling that is often associated with adolescence and an emotion that is quite difficult to display and acknowledge within the school environment. At a time when young people's hormones and bodily changes are creating new mood swings and experiences, strong feelings (whether of anger or another emotion) can be very confusing. However, enabling young people to explore the feelings of anger associated with grief and loss can be beneficial for teenagers.

Activity 8

Anger – Wild Animals Drama

Individual ☒   Group ☑

Materials

- Drum and rain stick
- Whiteboard and markers

Aims and Overview

- Drama is a powerful and useful way for young people to explore their anger. It is a physical, dramatic and expressive way of showing feelings as well as allowing a group experience, which can often be supportive.

- This dramatic exercise uses the imagination, asking the young people to visualise themselves as a wild animal and think about how they experience this in their body and their emotions. As animals, they are going to be asked to be aggressive and powerful, then safe and calm. The drum will be played during the first part of the exercise, to portray the aggressive aspect, and then the rain stick for the safe and calm part of the drama. This should help create the atmosphere. Although the term 'anger' is not used, being aggressive is one obvious way that some teenagers express anger. This exercise therefore allows them to feel anger and aggression safely, in the context of drama. It then directs them to calm down and feel safe, beginning a process of helping them to learn how to calm themselves down, if and when this is necessary.

- This exercise needs to be guided closely by the group leader. Other adults should also be present to support any young people who either become distressed or out of control, although this is unlikely.

Preparation

Ensure that the room is suitable, allowing for a generous distance between all members of the group as they move around or roll on the floor. A drama room or gym is ideal, but a large room is also suitable.

Page 1 of 3

Instructions

Introduce the exercise as an imagination exercise about wild animals. It is important to remind the group that at no time are they allowed to touch anyone else in the room: *this is a non-contact drama activity*. Have both drum and rain stick to hand. Then ask them to do the following:

- Find a space in the room and close your eyes.

- Imagine you are a wild animal, preferably a large, potentially aggressive one, such as a gorilla, tiger, lion, elephant, bear, or similar.

- Breathe deeply and think about what posture this animal would assume if it was feeling good, confident and as if it owned the world. Really express yourself as this animal through your body.

- Now open your eyes and feel yourself begin to prepare for moving around the room as this animal. Be aware of the others in the room. (Use the drum at this point.)

- When you are ready, begin to move around the room as your wild animal, feeling strong, confident and ready to take on any fight. You are invincible. Enjoy the feeling of moving around the room as the animal, strong and confident. Remember not to touch anyone.

- When you are ready, move into partners, so that you are standing in front of another young person being an animal. Look at this other animal, feel your body prepare to show aggression and confidence, and show your partner you cannot be beaten.

- Can you find a posture that shows your partner this? He or she will do the same for you. Remember, no touching.

- Now, move away from this partner. Walk around feeling strong and confident, pleased you have seen off an enemy.

- Move into your own space, slowly stop moving, and close your eyes. (Stop beating the drum at this point.)

- Using a few deep breaths, feel your body calm down and become less aggressive. Shake your arms and legs briefly to let any tension go. You are no longer in danger.

- Imagine now that you are content, peaceful and happy. You are in a room full of other animals of the same type, none of whom want to threaten you. You are safe.

- Open your eyes and look around. Prepare to walk around the room feeling safe and calm, knowing that each of the other animals in the room is a friend, and that no one will hurt you. (Use the rain stick at this point.)

- ◎ Look into the eyes of the other animals and feel the difference, now that you are content and peaceful.
- ◎ Slowly come to a stop again in your own space.
- ◎ Take a moment to find a final posture for how you feel as the animal now. (Finish using the rain stick here.)
- ◎ Now shake all feelings and thoughts of being an animal away: jump up and down, shake your arms and legs, shake your body, take one or two deep breaths, letting out all the leftover feelings of being an animal in a wild place, and returning to being yourself.
- ◎ Make sure you have let go of all feelings to do with being an animal. You are a young person again

Discussion

Gather the young people into a circle in the room. Facilitate a discussion for the young people on how they felt and what they did and did not enjoy about the exercise. Use the following prompts on the whiteboard:

- ◎ Did you enjoy being aggressive and confident?
- ◎ How did your body feel when you were aggressive and confident?
- ◎ When you were in partners, did you feel close to a fight, or ready to run, or frozen? Different people have different reactions to aggression.
- ◎ Was it easy to let go of the aggressive animal feelings and change to the calmer, happier ones?
- ◎ Did you enjoy being peaceful and calm?
- ◎ Are either of these feelings familiar to you in everyday life, or even occasionally?
- ◎ How did your body feel when you were happier?
- ◎ Finally, give the group time to think about what they have learnt about strong feelings and how they can affect our bodies and reactions to others. Link these feelings to experiences such as bereavement or other loss, if appropriate for the group.

Activity 9

Anger – Moulding My Anger

Individual ✔   *Group* ✔

Materials

- Air hardening clay; if not available, ceramic clay can be used as long as there is a kiln available to fire it at the end of the exercise
- Water supply
- An apron or old shirt for each person
- Whiteboard and markers

Aims and Overview

This exercise introduces working with clay to express feelings. It is a very messy but satisfying way of enabling feelings of anger around loss.

Preparation

Prepare the environment well. Ensure that the young people can get messy without any inhibitions, by wearing clothes for messy work, covered up by aprons or old shirts, and using a large, washable table. If this is a group exercise, choose carefully how many young people you wish to support at once. If it is a whole class activity, ensure there are helpers in the class to support any young people who become distressed, and make sure you know which young people have had recent bereavements or losses. Place vulnerable young people near to those they can trust or who are less vulnerable.

Instructions

Guide the group through the exercise as follows:

- This is an exercise to explore the feeling of anger as a result of loss. We will be using clay to express the anger.

- The main rules are that the clay remains on the table or desk, no one gets hurt, and (if working in a group) you do not interfere with someone else's work. If someone chooses to break these rules, they will be asked to leave the activity.

- Anger can be a difficult feeling. Some people get angry easily, some do not ever get angry. However, when someone experiences a loss, whether from a bereavement or another reason, anger is actually a normal feeling. This exercise can help you to express your anger safely and also control it if needed.

- Begin by picking up the piece of clay you have been given. Take your time to soften it, moulding it in your hands, making any shape you like, or just feeling it. Do you like the texture, the smell, the colour? Make sure you get to know it and allow it to feel soft in your hands. If it feels hard, you can add a bit of water to it to soften it.

- When you are ready, and feel you know your piece of clay, begin to think about something that has made you feel angry in the recent past. It can be something small or something big. Remember that, although this is an exercise about anger, we will make sure you do not feel angry when we finish.

- As you begin to feel the anger from your memory or thoughts, let it come into your hands, from your shoulders and down your arms.

- Breathe into your hands, and then allow your hands to make the shapes that they want to make. It could be cutting, chopping, knocking, pulling the clay, punching or it could be that a special shape emerges.

- Take your time to let the anger go into the clay and, as you do so, see if a shape emerges that becomes the angry shape for you. It could be flat, round, square, holey, a mess, a neat blob; there really is no right or wrong. Make sure you do not hurt yourself or damage anything while you are doing this. Anger can be a strong emotion.

- If you feel you need support at any time, either because your feelings overwhelm you or because you do not know what to do, ask your teacher or helper.

- We are going to spend about twenty minutes on this, but you can stop when you are ready.

- See if you can find a final shape that you would like to call your anger shape, and which really expresses your anger. This is a shape you can keep if you want to. Finish it any way you like. It will be kept for you when fired or left to harden.

- Now take a few deep breaths in and out. Each breath is letting out more of your anger, so that you are do not walk away still feeling angry. You have allowed yourself to be angry safely, something that can be very helpful when someone has experienced a significant loss.

Page 2 of 3

- When you are ready, clean up your hands and visualise the water washing away any last anger.
- Remember, if you have any thoughts or feelings as a result of this exercise, you can talk to one of your teachers or helpers.

Discussion

It is best to simply allow this to be an art exercise without a follow-on discussion. However, if you consider a discussion will be helpful to your group, use the following prompts:

- How do you usually express anger?
- Do you normally get angry?
- If you have had a recent loss, did your anger feel larger or smaller?
- How did you feel making the clay shapes?
- Does it help to know that anger is a normal feeling associated with loss?
- If you were feeling more angry at the beginning, did this exercise reduce your angry feelings?

Activity 10

Anger – The Shape of My Anger

Individual ✔   Group ✔

> **Materials**
> - Felt-tip pens, crayons and pencils
> - Whiteboard and markers
> - Worksheet 11, 'The Shape of My Anger' for each person

Aims and Overview

This exercise allows young people to use the anger shape on Worksheet 11 to express their feelings of anger within the shape. They can use writing, drawing or scribbling as an expression of their angry feelings. They can also tear it up and destroy it if they wish, particularly if there is something specific that makes them feel angry.

Preparation

- Ensure the atmosphere of the room is relaxed and feels safe enough for young people to begin to consider their feelings. Provide each young person with the worksheet. Have more worksheets available if necessary.

- Describe the exercise as one that gives them a safe way to express anger, using an angry shape to draw or scribble in. It can be helpful to explain to young people that allowing their anger out in this way can be very therapeutic, and can stop them reaching a stage of being violently angry or out of control with their anger.

- Remind the young people that anger is a feeling that is normally associated with loss, and it is fine to express anger in this context. Anger that spills out of control, such as anger which is damaging to property or people, however, is not acceptable in any circumstance.

Instructions

Guide the group through the exercise as follows:

- Think of a time when you were angry.
- Your anger could be about something that has happened or you can imagine how you feel when you are angry.
- Some people find this hard, others find it easy.
- Think of something you could put within the angry shape to express this feeling of anger that you have or imagine. If it is hard to think of something, consider writing the first words or phrases that come into your head, or doing a simple drawing or scribble.
- If you are angry with someone or about something that has happened, you can draw a picture of that person or incident and scribble it out. This does not hurt anyone but allows you to feel angry safely.
- If you have had a recent loss, anger is a normal feeling. This exercise may help you to cope with your feelings, without having to keep it in or let it out on others.
- When you are ready, take a red or a black pen and use it to colour over your angry shape until you cannot see the drawing or writing any more.
- If you want, you can then tear or screw up the paper and throw it in the bin. You are not saying that your anger is wrong, you are letting your angry feelings out safely.
- Do this as many times as you need to.
- At the end of the exercise, check how you feel. Are your angry feelings still there? If so, take a few deep breaths, letting some of the tension associated with anger out with each breath.
- If you need to speak to someone after this exercise, tell your teacher or another trusted adult.

Discussion

Prompts for a discussion after this exercise can include:

- Do you feel angry a lot of the time?
- Do you never feel angry?
- Has something happened to make you feel angry more?
- How do you normally show your anger? Or do you hide it away?

Activity 10: Anger – The Shape of My Anger

- What do you think is the best way to let anger out?
- Think of a few ways that can help you express anger (for example, doing sports activities, listening to loud music, going running, kicking a football).
- Did you find this exercise helpful?
- If yes, why? If no, why?
- Did you like the anger shape?
- Can you think of other shapes to express your anger also?

Activity 10

Worksheet 11

The Shape of My Anger

Activity 11

Anger – A Story of Loss

Individual ☒   Group ✔

Materials

◎ Worksheet 12, 'Excerpt from *Rory's Story* 1', for each young person

Aims and Overview

This exercise uses an excerpt from a story about loss, *Rory's Story*, and asks for young people's responses to various questions. The aim of the exercise is to allow them to reflect on Rory's feelings and consequent actions, and to reflect on times when they may have felt similarly. The discussion that results can be very helpful for all involved, as it can help older adolescents, in particular, to reflect on their feelings safely, without expressing or exposing them.

Preparation

◎ This exercise can take place in a school context (perhaps during citizenship classes or discussions on loss), or in a young people's bereavement group.

◎ It can be helpful to describe the exercise as being about loss and how people can get angry when they experience a serious loss.

Instructions and Discussion

Guide the group through the exercise as follows:

◎ Ask the young people to read through the scenario first.

◎ Then ask them to answer the questions honestly, if they can.

◎ Facilitate a group discussion using the questions as prompts.

Activity 11

Worksheet 12

Excerpt from *Rory's Story* (1)

He trudged back to where they were playing, hearing in his head the sounds of shouts and mocking, and suddenly he saw red and flashed with a violence he had not felt before. He felt angry at them for spitting him out of the gang, just because his mum had died. He felt angry at her for going and leaving him, at his dad for not being there for him and not understanding, at his big sister for not letting him stay off school, at the teachers who tried to be kind and actually made it worse by telling the whole class how his mum had sadly passed away after a heart attack – what did it mean? What was he meant to do now?

He moved faster, raging inside with the violence and unfairness of it all, and suddenly he realised he wanted to escape from it all, escape from the pain, the anger and the school, escape to a freedom where it would never hurt again, where his world could never again be turned on its head like this.

Excerpt from Jacobs, *Rory's Story: a Teenager's Story of Loss*, 2014

Questions:

1. Have you ever felt like this? When? What did you do about it?

2. If you have never felt like this, can you imagine what it might feel like? What might you do about it?

3. Do you think Rory was right to feel like this?

4. How many ways is Rory saying he is angry? Are they all good reasons for being angry?

5. Discuss in your group what Rory may need to help him with his feelings of anger.

6. What do you think is acceptable to show when you feel angry? Do you agree or disagree with what others say in your group?

Sadness

Sadness can be a difficult feeling during adolescence. It leaves young people feeling vulnerable at a time when they are prone to deep and fluctuating emotions due to their stage of development, and it can lead them to feel out of control at a time when their hormones and bodily changes are creating new mood swings and experiences. However, allowing young people to explore the feelings of sadness associated with grief and loss can be both beneficial and enhance their emotional development.

Activity 12

Sadness – Drawing My Sadness

Individual ✔   Group ✔

Materials

- Paper, palettes and paintbrushes for each young person
- Paints and water
- Copies of images from other artists such as Vincent Van Gogh, whose paintings could be seen to represent sadness (See Resources, 'Music, Poetry and Art Resources', for more ideas)
- Whiteboard and markers

Aims and Overview

- This is an art exercise. Art is one of the best ways of expressing feelings for teenagers, and can be very individual and expressive without revealing too much personal detail. This is therefore experienced as a 'safe' exercise for most young people.

- Young people will be asked to paint and draw images, patterns or colours which they associate with the feeling of sadness. They will need encouragement to understand that there is no wrong or right way to represent this feeling, and that they can choose themselves how to show it. By showing them other images created by different artists, it should be possible to give them ideas of how to show their feelings by painting.

- If there are young people in the group who have experienced loss in the recent past, monitor if they wish to do this exercise and offer them support if necessary.

Preparation

- Ensure the room is suitable for art activities, either by protecting furniture or using an art room where it is possible to create artwork safely. Also ensure that the atmosphere in the room is one of safety, so that difficult feelings can be explored. There is a final step to the exercise which will help dispel any leftover feelings of sadness.

- Provide each young person with paper, paints, palettes and paintbrushes.

- ◉ Allow up to an hour for the art exercise and sharing afterwards.
- ◉ Try to ensure that any particularly vulnerable young people, such as those who have recently experienced loss or bereavement, or who are known to be vulnerable for other reasons, are seated near supportive peers or close to a teacher or teaching assistant they can turn to if needed.

Instructions

Guide the group through the exercise as follows:

- ◉ Today we are going to use art to explore sadness.
- ◉ Think of any times when you have felt sad, for example reading a book, watching a film or DVD, or for a personal reason.
- ◉ If you cannot remember any times of feeling sad, try to imagine what it feels like.
- ◉ How might you represent this sadness in art form?
- ◉ Think about the colour or colours, the shapes and the images you could use.
- ◉ You could, for example, paint a proper picture, a blob of colour or colours, stick people, add words, or do a design or scribble picture. These are just some ideas. You may have your own.
- ◉ There are a few images up on the board to show you how others have expressed sadness in art.
- ◉ Remember there is no right or wrong today. This is not an art class. It is about using art to express feelings. There is a big difference.
- ◉ At the end, we will ask if anyone wants to show their painting to the group and describe what it is about. You do not have to do this if you do not want to. It is your choice.
- ◉ When you are ready, start your painting. Try not to think of it as something you have to get right. It is OK to make mistakes, try different things and mix colours. There are enough paints for everyone.
- ◉ You will have up to an hour for painting and sharing.
- ◉ If you have any questions, or need extra support, or become upset, come and tell us so that we can help.
- ◉ When we have finished, we will look at the pictures as a group, and you can choose if you want to say something about yours.
- ◉ Don't be surprised if the room goes quiet and a bit gloomy. We will finish with an exercise to shake the feelings of sadness out of our bodies.

Discussion

Use the following prompts for any discussion and follow-up activities:

- Was painting a good way to express your feeling of sadness?
- How did you feel while doing the painting? Less or more sad?
- Was this OK or not?
- Is sadness an OK feeling to show with friends?
- Do you cry after a film or do you ever cry alone? Is this real sadness?
- Do you think crying helps when we feel sad?
- How else could we express feelings of sadness?
- If you have had a loss either recently or in the past, did this art exercise help with any feelings of sadness?

Letting Go

Before everyone leaves, ask the group to stand up and shake the sad feeling out of their bodies: this can be done by waving arms, shaking legs, moving the body and having some fun, even some dancing if needed. Remind them that they are doing this to release any leftover feelings of sadness, as all feelings are felt physically as well as emotionally.

Activity 13

Sadness – Drama Exercise

Individual ☒   Group ☑

Materials

- Cushions and blankets
- Music to support the drama (see Resources, 'Music, Poetry & Art Resources', or choose your own piece of music)
- Whiteboard and markers

Aims and Overview

- Emotions such as sadness and anger are felt very physically within the body. This is an exercise that asks young people to express themselves physically while exploring emotions. Sadness is an emotion that young people can have particular difficulty with.

- Make sure that everyone knows they do not have to join in for the whole exercise, but encourage them to at least start it.

- Also remind them that if they feel distress at any point, they can ask for extra help. Have a few extra helpers such as teaching assistants nearby, if possible.

Preparation

- Ensure the room is large enough for a group of young people to spread out safely, but comfortable enough for them to be on the floor. Spread the cushions and blankets around the edges of the room for those who might want to use them.

- Ensure that the room feels safe and relaxed and that the young people understand the exercise before they start.

Instructions

Guide the group through the exercise as follows:

- Today we are going to explore the feeling of sadness. All of you will have probably had this feeling at some point. This could be due to a loss you have experienced or from some other cause, such as watching a sad movie or reading a sad book, or simply just hearing sad news from someone.
- Find a place in the room where you are alone. Spread your arms out wide so that you know you cannot touch another person.
- When you are ready, try and find a posture that, for you, expresses the feeling of sadness. It can be standing, lying, bending, or stretching. There is no wrong or right way.
- Take a moment to feel this emotion, even if it is a little uncomfortable.
- Does this feeling give your body energy, or make you feel tired?
- Is it a good or a difficult feeling?
- And does your body want to stay in this posture, or move away from it fast?
- Now, break from this posture by jumping up and down and shaking your arms and legs vigorously.
- Release the feeling of sadness and replace it with the opposite, a feeling of happiness.
- Find a posture for being happy. See how different your body shape is and feel yourself into it.
- When you are ready, ask yourself the same questions as before.
- Does this feeling give your body energy, or make you feel tired?
- Is it a good or a difficult feeling?
- And does your body want to stay in this posture or move away from it fast?
- Then shake this posture away and return briefly to the sad posture.
- Does it feel different now, or the same as before?
- Is it easier or more difficult to find the sad posture, now you have felt the happy posture?
- One last time, shake out the sad posture and return to the happy posture.
- Give yourself a minute to breath in the happy posture, then return to a normal pose.
- When you are ready, sit down, so we can talk as a group about how you felt.

Discussion

Encourage the group to think about and discuss the following points:

- Sadness nearly always feels tiring and draining of energy. This is why people who are depressed are often tired much of the time. Feeling loss and grief also has the same effect, though this is usually temporary.

- It is possible to change the way we feel or control the depth of our feelings. Even though we cannot change the circumstances if we feel loss and sadness, we can sometimes choose how sad to be and when.

- We were able to move from sad to happy twice in a short space of time – was this easy? Was it possible? This shows you that if you feel stuck in one emotion, it is possible to change it, although it may take some time to change it permanently.

- Did the happy feeling seem more energising? There is now a psychology called 'happiness psychology' (see *The Psychology of Happiness*, 2001 for further details). This is based on the idea that the more we feel happy, the more we can feel good about ourselves and the more we can achieve the things we want in life as we get older.

- It is not wrong to feel sad. There are often good reasons for feeling sad. But it is also OK to try and feel happy and not to dwell on being sad.

Activity 14

Sadness – Questions about Sadness

Individual ✔   *Group* ✔

Materials

- Worksheet 13, 'Questions about Sadness', for each person
- Pens and/or pencils

Aims and Overview

This exercise allows young people to reflect on what it is that makes them feel sad by asking questions related to sadness. It enables them to consider these thoughts privately and then discuss them publicly in their group if they choose. It also allows the group to consider that all young people feel sad, but sometimes there are particular events, such as death and divorce, a person moving away or going to prison, which cause extra sadness.

Preparation

- Ensure that the group is in a relaxed and safe environment in which difficult feelings such as sadness can be explored. Discuss briefly the subject of loss and grief, and how sadness is a normal and typical feeling resulting from loss.

- If there are young people in the group who have experienced a significant loss in the past, check that they are sitting where they can gain extra support if needed, and remind them that they can ask for help or to speak to someone at any point in the exercise.

Instructions

Describe the exercise for the group as one in which they will be asked some questions related to sadness on a worksheet. Ask them to answer in writing as honestly as they can, but mention that they can then choose what they wish to share in a discussion at the end.

Activity 14

Worksheet 13

Questions about Sadness

Below are a number of questions related to sadness. When you are ready, write as many answers as you can in the spaces. Try and be truthful. At the end, your teacher will help you to discuss your answers in your group or on your own.

What makes you feel sad? Think of some things that have made you feel sad in the past or recently.

_____
_____
_____

Does reading a sad book make you feel sad? Can you name a book you read that made you feel sad?

_____
_____
_____

Does watching a movie or DVD make you sad? Can you name a film or describe a scene that made you feel sad recently?

_____
_____
_____

Page 1 of 3

Worksheet 13: Questions about Sadness

Can you name something that you have thought of which makes you feel sad? How do you express this?

_____
_____
_____

Are you comfortable feeling sad? Some people are OK with feeling sad and others find it hard to be sad. Which are you? Do you know why?

_____
_____
_____

Does remembering something that has happened to you make you feel sad? Can you say something about the thing that you remember?

_____
_____
_____

Does bad weather such as rain or a thunderstorm make you feel sad sometimes? If so, can you remember the last time this happened?

_____
_____
_____

Do you ever feel sad when something upsetting happens in your family? Can you remember anything at all that made you feel sad and happened in your family?

_____
_____
_____

Do you ever feel sad when something upsetting happens with your friends? Can you remember anything that made you feel sad that happened with your friends?

_____

_____

_____

When you feel sad, what do you do? If you never feel sad, can you imagine what you would do if you did?

_____

_____

_____

Now, when you have answered all the questions that you can, can you answer a final one?

What helps when you feel sad? Can you name three things that help you to feel less sad? If you do not get sad, then it is all right to just imagine what might help.

_____

_____

_____

At the end of this exercise, your teacher will ask you if there is anything from any of the questions that you would like to tell the others about. If you do not wish to do this, that is fine, as this is a private exercise to help you to think about feeling sad, which happens to us all at some time in our lives. Some of you may want a discussion and your teacher can help to support this.

Activity 15

Sadness – Poetry & Sadness

Individual ✔   Group ✔

Materials

- Worksheet 14, 'Suggested Sad Poems', for each young person; alternatively you can prepare your own poetry choices to use as worksheets
- Paper, pens and/or pencils for each person
- Whiteboard for keywords; markers

Aims and Overview

- Poetry is an excellent way to express all emotions, but particularly so for sadness. This exercise allows the young people to first listen to some poetry expressing sadness, then to write their own poem.

- Worksheet 14 contains two sad poems that may be read out, but if you prefer your own choices or have favourites, you can use these instead (see also Resources, 'Music, Poetry & Art Resources', for further suggested poets).

Preparation

- Gather together some poems on sadness, either using Worksheet 14 or of your own choosing.

- Write the following keywords on the board: dark, wet, low, longing, pain, blue, clouds, tears, damp, struggle, flow, night, cry, dull, murmur, slow.

- Ensure that the room feels relaxed and calm. Remember to check if any of the young people have had a recent significant loss and that these people are sitting where they need to, either near friends or where they feel safe enough to consider their sad feelings.

Page 1 of 3

Instructions

Introduce the session by explaining that this is an exercise to explore the feeling of sadness through poetry. Poetry is traditionally a form of expression that can show many feelings and thoughts, and today the group is going to think of sadness as related to loss and grief. If anyone has no experience of loss, they could try to imagine how it would feel.

Guide the group through the exercise as follows:

- Read the poems out to the group before giving them the worksheets, as listening is a particular way of experiencing a poem.
- Hand out the copies of the poems and allow group members time to read them.
- Ask the group how the poems made them feel. Were they a true expression of sadness for them?
- Mention that different people react to poetry very differently, so it is all right not to feel the same as the others in the group.
- Explain what a poem is: a small, creative piece of writing, usually in short lines, occasionally rhyming, which expresses a particular thought, memory or feeling.
- Tell the group that it is now their turn to try and write their poems on sadness, and that there are a number of words on the board that may help.
- Assure them that they can take their time.
- Suggest that the first step is to think of something that makes them sad.
- Then they can try to make up a few sentences that could express the feeling of sadness, using the words on the board if this helps.
- When they have written enough sentences, they can try and make them into a poem.
- Remind them that they can ask for help whenever they need to, either with their poems or if they begin to feel upset.
- Tell the group that there will be a poetry reading at the end for anyone who wants to share their poem.
- Explain that the group poetry reading will be followed by a brief discussion about how they experienced the exercise, and if they would use poetry writing as a way to help them if they ever feel sad.
- At the end of the session the group can choose together what to do with the poems, either putting them on the wall or in a small book.

Discussion

These questions can help to stimulate a group discussion and may be written up on the board:

- Did listening to the poetry affect how you felt?
- Did writing the poem affect how you felt?
- Did you agree that the other poems, written by the group members, were sad poems?
- What words are particularly sad for you?
- Would you write a poem again?

Activity 15

Worksheet 14

Suggested Sad Poems

Do not Stand at My Grave and Weep

Do not stand at my grave and weep,

I am not there; I do not sleep.

I am a thousand winds that blow,

I am the diamond glints on snow,

I am the sunlight on ripened grain,

I am the gentle autumn rain.

When you awaken in the morning's hush

I am the swift uplifting rush

Of quiet birds in circled flight.

I am the soft stars that shine at night.

Do not stand at my grave and cry.

I am not there; I did not die.

Mary Elizabeth Frye, 1932

The Shadow on the Stone

I went by the Druid stone
    That broods in the garden white and lone,
And I stopped and looked at the shifting shadows
    That at some moments fall thereon
    From the tree hard by with a rhythmic swing,
    And they shaped in my imagining
To the shade that a well-known head and shoulders
    Threw there when she was gardening.

    I thought her behind my back,
Yea, her I long had learned to lack,
And I said: 'I am sure you are standing behind me,
    Though how do you get into this old track?'
    And there was no sound but the fall of a leaf
    As a sad response; and to keep down grief
I would not turn my head to discover
    That there was nothing in my belief.

    Yet I wanted to look and see
That nobody stood at the back of me;
But I thought once more: 'Nay, I'll not unvision
    A shape which, somehow, there may be.'
    So I went on softly from the glade,
    And left her behind me throwing her shade,
As she were indeed an apparition—
    My head unturned lest my dream should fade.

Thomas Hardy, 1917 (from *The Complete Poems*, 2001)

Activity 16

Sadness – A Story of Loss

Individual ✗   *Group* ✓

> **Materials**
>
> ⊚ Worksheet 15, 'Excerpt from *Rory's Story* (2)', for each young person

Aims and Overview

This exercise describes a scenario and asks for young people's responses to various questions. The aim of the exercise is to allow them to reflect on their feelings, and to reflect on times when they may have felt similarly. It can also help build empathy for those who are experiencing loss or bereavement by helping young people think about how their peers may feel if this happens to them.

Preparation

⊚ This exercise can take place during discussions on loss, or within a bereavement context in a group of bereaved young people.

⊚ It can be helpful to describe the exercise as being about loss and how people can feel sad when they experience a serious loss. Check that if young people in a group have actually been bereaved of a loved one they are ready to share their feelings and do this exercise. Those who are recently bereaved should not do this exercise.

Instructions

⊚ Ask the young people to read through the scenario first.

⊚ Then ask them to think about the questions that follow the excerpt and decide what their own answers would be.

⊚ Emphasise that they should try to be as honest with themselves as they feel able, but that there are no right or wrong answers.

Discussion

Use the questions on Worksheet 15 as prompts to encourage a group discussion about feelings of deep sadness and how someone might support a friend who was feeling very sad because of a significant loss.

Activity 16

Worksheet 15

Excerpt from *Rory's Story* (2)

His mum – he had thought about her again and it came pouring back into his drained and empty head and he could feel it like an empty, dark, stabbing hole in his heart, this place where his mum used to be and he could hardly breathe with it. What was he doing here, what should he do now, he was alone in the world, all alone and she had left him, gone and left him, damn her, and he doubled up with the pain of it.

Excerpt from Jacobs, *Rory's Story: a Teenager's Story of Loss*, 2014

Questions

- Have you ever felt like this? When? What did you do about it?

- If you have never felt like this, can you imagine what it might feel like? What might you do about it?

- Discuss in your group what support Rory may need for his deep sadness.

- Have you ever lost a family member? Can you remember how you felt?

- How did you let your sad feelings out?

- If you felt like this, what support would you want? Would you want to be left alone?

Fear & Anxiety

Fear and anxiety are a normal part of growing up, and young people will naturally have some fears typical of their stage of emotional development, such as the fear of losing friends, of being made to seem different or stupid in front of others, and the fear of bullying or not being part of a group. They may have very real fears about their developing bodies, or fears about their developing sexuality. The additional pressure of loss and grief can cause these fears to seem excessive and huge in the minds of vulnerable young people. Therefore helping to support these vulnerable young people in particular, and offering exercises to explore fears and anxiety to all young people, can help those who are vulnerable as a result of loss to gain support and begin to talk about their feelings and needs safely.

The following exercises allow young people to begin to share their fears and anxieties with each other. They also allow those who have experienced significant bereavement or loss to begin to make sense of their loss and the fears and anxiety that have resulted from this. It can be reassuring for them to realise that all young people have some fears and anxiety, whether or not they have experienced a significant loss.

Activity 17

Fear & Anxiety – Causes of Fear

Individual ☒   Group ☑

Materials

- Pens and/or pencils for each young person
- Worksheet 16, 'Fear', for each person

Aims and Overview

- This exercise is a group exercise to enable young people to explore together what it is that causes fear, and to find some ways to support them in their experience of fear. Although most of the prompts and questions are not directly related to grief and loss, the discussion after the exercise can be linked to related issues, such as bereavement, divorce or other forms of loss.
- The group will be asked to respond to a series of questions on a sheet; each one can inform a discussion, but there is also a short list of prompts to encourage further sharing about fear.

Preparation

Remember to prepare in advance, in particular by making the room a welcoming and relaxing environment. Young people who are either experiencing fear or reminded of their fears, will respond better if they are relaxed and feel safe.Instructions

- Introduce the topic of fear by asking if any young person in the group has ever experienced being afraid. Most young people feel such emotions during their time as teenagers.
- Allow for a small general discussion on fear before they do the exercise.
- Describe the exercise as one that will ask them to answer questions on a worksheet related to fear. When they have filled in as many answers as they can, they will then have a general discussion on some of these answers.

Page 1 of 2

◎ Give them Worksheet 16 and allow at least twenty minutes for the teenagers to write their answers, before you have a discussion.

◎ Arrange for extra support in the room, if possible, such as from teaching assistants.

◎ Remind the group that they can ask questions or request support at any time, and that the aim of this exercise is to encourage a discussion of fear and to help them remember the things that can support them when they do have these feelings.

Activity 17

Worksheet 16

Fear

Answer each question as much as you want to. Try and answer every question. If you get upset at any point, tell a teacher or another trusted adult.

Have you ever felt afraid? Give examples.
_____
_____
_____

Have you ever wanted to run away? If so, when and why? Give examples.
_____
_____
_____

Have you ever wanted to protect someone so much you would put yourself at risk? When and why?
_____
_____
_____

Have you ever felt frozen in fear? What caused this?
_____
_____
_____

Do you have a fear of something in particular? Do you have any reason for this fear? (For example, people are afraid of flying or of spiders, but have never had a bad experience.) Are you able to say what your fear is?

_____

_____

_____

Do you know what you would do in the event of a disaster befalling you or your family?

_____

_____

_____

What is your automatic reaction when you feel afraid, for example when watching a movie?

_____

_____

_____

Do you sometimes enjoy feeling afraid, for example on a white-knuckle ride at a fair?

_____

_____

_____

What do you think happens in your body when you feel afraid?

_____

_____

_____

When you have felt fear, does it remain in your body or does it eventually go? What helps it to go?

_____
_____
_____

Did you know that fear is felt very physically? For example, it is known that people have a 'flight or fight' reaction to fear. There are other common reactions. Can you think of two of them?

_____
_____
_____

What helps you to feel less afraid? Give examples.

_____
_____
_____

Discussion

Think about the following things and try to discuss them in the group:

- Does thinking about fear make it worse or better?
- What was it like writing about some of your fears and reactions?
- Things that help: using calming breath, counting to ten, telling someone, distraction by doing something nice.

Activity 18

Fear & Anxiety – Drama Exercise

Individual ☒　　　Group ☑

Materials

- Small drum or tambourine

Aims and Overview

- This exercise allows young people to feel fear safely and to explore how to manage it. It is an imaginative exercise using drama and you will be giving the group instructions.

- Prepare for a discussion after the exercise, to allow the young people to explore how it felt and how their bodies reacted. Remind them that the flight, fight or freeze reaction is the norm when fear is experienced, and anxiety is a moderated version of this.

- Ensure that there are helpers available for if the exercise stimulates stronger reactions, and if there are any young people in your group who are particularly vulnerable due to recent losses, ensure they are well supported.

Preparation

- Ensure the room is large enough for a group of young people to move around safely.

- Prepare the young people by talking about fears and anxiety and reminding them that fears and anxiety are normal when people experience grief and loss. Though this exercise is not directly related to loss, it is certainly related to fear.

- Fear and anxiety are emotions that are felt very physically. Therefore exploring these through the medium of drama can be very helpful for anyone who is experiencing fears or anxiety at any level.

- Allow at least twenty minutes for the drama exercise.

- Make sure the drum is nearby when you begin the drama exercise. Tell the young people that the drum will signify a scary monster.

Instructions

Guide the group through the exercise as follows:

- If anyone is upset during this exercise, they can stop at any point and ask for help from a teacher or helper.
- Find a place in the room where you can spread your arms out on both sides and not touch anyone.
- You can stand or sit. Imagine that where you are standing or sitting is the safest, best place in the world for you. You are at peace and nothing can harm you. Enjoy this for a moment.
- Now, imagine that a huge, aggressive monster is going to come bursting into the room – you know it is there, but you don't know what to do. This is the beginning of fear.
- Without moving from the spot where you are in the room, how does your body react? What posture does your body want to make to show this fear? Hold this posture for a short while.
- How is your breathing? Slow, fast, tense?
- Now, forget the monster, as he has chosen not to come into the room after all.
- Can you shake the fear and the posture you felt out of your body? Can you do a few deep breaths to relax?
- Return to that sense of being safe and secure, and with nothing nearby to harm you. Enjoy this again.
- Now think of something you are actually afraid of, but do not choose a big fear that is really scary. Think of a small fear.
- Then do the same thing, find a posture with your body and a shape that expresses this fear. Is it the same one as before, or a different one?
- Again, let go of this fear, return to the sense of feeling safe and secure in your spot, and shake your body back to normal. There is nothing to be afraid of.
- For the last bit of our drama exercise we are going to move around. The main rule to remember is to respect each other and not to touch. There is enough space for everyone.
- You are going to leave the spot where you feel safe and secure. Remember where it is so you can return to it at the end.
- Start by walking around slowly, then a bit faster. Just look around, still feeling fairly relaxed and safe.
- When the drum starts to beat, imagine that the monster is back and this time he is in the room.

- The monster is roaming around the room looking for a victim. It is very scary.
- It is dangerous and you need to hide or avoid him. Move around, trying to find a place to be safe. You can run or walk but do not bump into other people.
- When the drum stops beating, stop where you are. Find the posture that describes how you feel now, afraid and trying to escape. Hold this posture. Check how your breathing is and your body.
- Then slowly release your posture, move again and find your safe place. The monster has slunk away, and is not going to attack you after all. He is gone.
- Return to the place you began, and calm yourself. You are once again safe and secure, and nothing will get you.
- Find the posture to describe how you feel now. Hold it and watch how your breathing feels.

Discussion

When everyone is ready, form a circle to discuss the exercise and what our body feels when we feel fear. The following are useful prompts to encourage discussion:

- Was it easy or not to feel safe in this exercise?
- Was it easy or not to feel fear in this exercise?
- What was the difference in your body?
- Was it easy to calm down after feeling fear?
- How did you do this?
- Some typical symptoms of fear in our bodies are: tension, extra sweat, breath quickening, being on hyper-alert and watchful, a rigid body, and a desire to run, freeze, attack, or defend.
- Some typical ways to calm down after feeling fear: taking a few deep breaths; walking slowly; thinking of something relaxing and safe; telling someone; or shaking or moving our body vigorously to remove tension.
- Stress and anxiety have similar effects on our bodies.
- Did the group enjoy this exercise? If yes, why? If not, why?
- Do you thinking practising feeling fear will help in real-life situations? Some people, such as those who work in accident and emergency departments, are naturally more able to manage emergencies than others. Is this because of practice?
- What kind of impact do you think fear has on those who do dangerous jobs daily, for example soldiers, firemen?

Activity 19

Fear & Anxiety – Reflections

Individual ✔   *Group* ✔

> **Materials**
>
> ◎ Worksheets 17 & 18, 'Anxiety in My Life' and 'Dealing with Anxiety', for each person

Aims and Overview

◎ This exercise focuses on anxieties related to loss. Young people typically have many anxieties and worries during their teenage years, and anxieties stemming from grief and loss can be a part of these. This exercise allows young people to begin to reflect on their anxieties and how to manage them or who to tell if they have extreme anxieties.

◎ Young people are asked to fill in boxes on Worksheet 17 that relate to different parts of their life and to draw or write something about their anxieties and worries. Then they are asked to fill in the boxes on Worksheet 18 to identify what helps when they become anxious or worried. The teacher then supports a discussion to help them share some solutions and, if they wish, some of their worries.

◎ This exercise is suitable for all young people, but can also be undertaken with a group of teenagers who have all experienced loss.

Preparation

Prepare the young people by asking them to consider any anxieties or worries they may have. Ensure the room is safe and relaxed enough for them to think of these aspects of their life. Place vulnerable young people close to friends or others who can support them. Give time to help them think of their anxieties safely, and ensure that there are support staff or other workers available if needed.

Instructions

Guide the group through the exercise as follows:

- All young people experience anxieties and worries at some point in their lives. When you also experience a loss, these anxieties can grow.

- Some anxieties will be ones that you all have, such as that you look OK and have friends. Other anxieties may be very personal and related to your experiences and life.

- Although this is an exercise primarily about anxieties resulting from loss, you can use it for other anxieties too.

- On Worksheet 17 are various boxes that stand for the different parts of your life.

- Look at these boxes and write down or draw any anxieties or worries you have in the boxes (or parts of your life) that are most important to you.

- When you have filled in all the boxes you want to, decide if you would like to tell someone about them, or how you manage them.

- Then look at the Worksheet 18 and fill in all the ways you are supported in managing your anxieties.

- You can then talk about the two exercises as a group if you wish.

Activity 19

Worksheet 17

Anxiety in My Life

Home life

Family relations

School life

Page 1 of 4

Worksheet 17: Anxiety in My Life

Friends

Schoolwork

Outside activities

Behaviour

Food

Sleeping

Relationships (for example, with a girlfriend/boyfriend)

Physical appearance

Other

[ ]

What helps your worries and anxieties?

[ ]

Remember to tell someone if any of your anxieties are large enough to affect daily life.

Worksheet 17: Anxiety in My Life

Activity 19

Worksheet 18

Dealing with Anxiety

When I feel anxious I can tell:

- [ ] A parent
- [ ] My teacher
- [ ] My carer
- [ ] My pet
- [ ] My friends
- [ ] My friends on computer
- [ ] My neighbour
- [ ] My family/brother/sister
- [ ] My teaching assistant
- [ ] My girlfriend/boyfriend
- [ ] No one
- [ ] Other _____

When I feel anxious I may:

- [ ] Tell someone
- [ ] Watch television
- [ ] Go out
- [ ] Play computer games
- [ ] Play music
- [ ] Other _____
- [ ] Sit and read
- [ ] Sit quietly and speak to no one
- [ ] Use the computer
- [ ] Do sports such as football
- [ ] Write/draw
- [ ] Do nothing

Page 1 of 2

When I feel anxious I need:

- [ ] Someone to talk to
- [ ] To be left alone
- [ ] Someone to give me a cuddle
- [ ] Someone to help me forget
- [ ] A warm drink
- [ ] A nice meal
- [ ] Help

- [ ] Sleep
- [ ] To go out and have some fun
- [ ] My friends nearby
- [ ] To know I am not to blame
- [ ] To be with my cat/dog/pet
- [ ] My family all around me
- [ ] Other _____

Discussion

Think about the following things and discuss them with the group:

- Does telling someone help when you are anxious?
- Different people have different ways of coping; share your own ways of coping with the group.
- Do some people in the group have anxieties in common?
- Are there some experiences in life that are more anxiety-provoking?
- How did you experience the exercise? Was it helpful, or not?

Happiness

It is very important for young people to remember that feeling happy is important, and this is particularly so when they have experienced a bereavement or a loss. Feeling good and happy can help strengthen a young person's ability to manage difficult times. This can enhance teenager's self-esteem and self-confidence and build resilience for young people, which can be really important for those who have experienced loss.

The exercises following remind young people of times when they feel happy, help them to find ways to be happy and encourage them to be happy even in the midst of quite difficult life experiences.

Activity 20

Happiness – What Makes You Happy? (1)

Individual ✔   Group ✔

Materials

- Worksheet 19, 'Feeling Happy', for each young person

Aims and Overview

- This exercise is to help young people feel that it is OK to be happy, even when difficult things are happening, such as the experience of loss.

- Worksheet 19 asks young people three simple questions to remind them how to be happy and what helps them feel happy.

Preparation

- Decide if this should be an individual exercise for someone who has experienced loss, or a group exercise.

- Ensure that the group experience takes place in a relaxed environment where the young people can reflect on their experience. If the group is particularly about loss, this exercise can be introduced as one to help remind them that being happy is still an important part of life.

Instructions and Discussion

- Introduce the exercise and ask the young person or group to think about what makes them happy. Then ask them to fill in the worksheet. Give up to twenty minutes for this part of the exercise.

- Offer an opportunity for discussion if a group is undertaking the exercise.

- Discussion aid: there is further information in the Resources section about the way in which feeling happy actually supports health and intelligence.

Activity 20

Worksheet 19

Feeling Happy

What helps you to feel happy? Draw or write something about the things that make you feel happy.

Is there a place you go to that helps you feel happy? For example: the seaside, to a relative's house, an imaginary place, or to visit friends. Draw or write about this. If you do not have an actual place to visit, imagine a place that makes you feel happy.

Page 1 of 2

Is there something special you do that helps keep you feeling happy? Or do you imagine doing something that makes you happy? Draw or write about this.

Think about the following things and discuss them in your group:

- Is being happy the same as having fun?

- Is it every person's right to feel happy?

- If not, why not?

- If anyone doing the exercise has experienced loss, have they found it harder or easier to feel happy?

- Do you know that feeling happy actually helps boost your health and intelligence?

- What would it be like if you had lessons on happiness at school?

Activity 21

Happiness – What Makes You Happy? (2)

Individual ✔   Group ✔

Materials

- Worksheet 20, 'What Makes You Happy?', for each person.

Aims and Overview

This exercise aims to help young people, particularly those who have experienced loss, to remember that being happy is important. It offers a list of ways that it is possible to feel happy, and asks them to tick which activities from the list they are familiar with. It also gives them future suggestions of how to feel happy.

Preparation

- Decide if this should be an individual exercise for someone who has experienced loss, or a group exercise.

- Ensure that the group experience takes place in a relaxed environment where the young people can reflect on their experience. If the group is particularly about loss, this exercise can be introduced as one to remind them that being happy is still an important part of life.

Instructions and Discussion

- Groups can be given the opportunity to discuss how important they think feeling happy is at the end of the exercise.

- Discussion aid: for further information about the way in which happiness can affect the body, look at *The Endorphin Effect* (Bloom, 2001).

Activity 21

Worksheet 20

What Makes You Happy?

Tick any of the following things that help you feel happy. Add your own suggestions at the end.

- [ ] Listening to music
- [ ] Reading a good book
- [ ] Watching a good film
- [ ] Going out with friends
- [ ] Eating a nice meal
- [ ] Going for a nice walk
- [ ] Going out to a special place
- [ ] Going out with special friends
- [ ] Spending time with family
- [ ] Meditating silently
- [ ] Singing out loud
- [ ] Dancing, any style
- [ ] Watching nature
- [ ] Doing a particular hobby
- [ ] Doing a sport

- [ ] Making something
- [ ] Painting, drawing or writing something
- [ ] Doing exercise, such as running or biking
- [ ] Gardening
- [ ] Going on the computer
- [ ] Playing computer games
- [ ] Going on holiday
- [ ] Thinking of something nice
- [ ] Going shopping
- [ ] _____
- [ ] _____
- [ ] _____
- [ ] _____

Discussion

Think about the following things and discuss them in your group:

- Is happiness important?
- What happens when people are not happy for a long time?
- What are the favourite ways to feel happy?
- What are the least favourite ways to feel happy?
- Does this change depending on the age of the people?
- How hard is it to feel happy when something difficult happens in your life?
- Is it hard not to feel guilty about being happy when others are not happy?
- If you have lost someone, what would that person say to you about being happy?
- Who are your role models for staying happy?
- Happiness affects the body profoundly. Do you know about the effect of endorphins? Discuss this and other ways that happiness can affect you physically.

Activity 22

Happiness – Music & Happiness

Individual ☒   Group ☑

Materials

- A range of percussion instruments, enough for everyone in the group. Try to ensure lots of variety: shakers, tambourines, drums, rain sticks, triangles, bells, and so on.

Aims and Overview

- This exercise shows how music can affect our emotions. Percussion instruments offer a fun and rhythmic way to experience the joy of sounds. In this exercise, a group of young people will play together, which leads to a group experience of having fun and feeling happy.

- During the activity each young person is given a chance to be in charge of the group, which allows them to choose the rhythm or tempo and also the sound level.

- The discussion at the end can cover the effect of music on how young people feel, and how important it is to feel happy at times.

Preparation

- This exercise is best done in a large space such as a hall or music room. It is a noisy and fun exercise, so ensure you are in a room in which you will not disturb others.

- Ensure that the young people know the signals during the exercise, so that you can remain in charge. A nod of the head, a whistle or a loud drum could all be used depending on the size of the group, the situation and how easy you think it will be for them to notice your signals.

Instructions

Guide the group through the exercise as follows:

- Today we are going to use the instruments to explore being happy.
- Choose an instrument. There enough to go around for everyone.
- Form a circle in the room so we can all see each other with the instruments. Perhaps it would be most relaxing if everyone sits on the floor while we play?
- As they are percussion instruments, we may be quite loud, so please keep looking at me as we play.
- Now, before we start, see if you can feel happiness inside you.
- Feel the happy feeling bubbling up from your toes through your body into your hands.
- Now we are all going to start together, following me. I will be in charge of the rhythm to begin with. Then you will each have a turn. My signal to change things will be [describe the signal].
- First, let's just play the instruments together, as loudly as we can.
- Now, let's go a bit quieter.
- When I make my signal, each person will take it in turns to control the rhythm, making it slow or fast, loud or quiet.
- I will finish by being in charge again.
- [Let each person in the group have a turn at controlling the speed of the rhythm, some will be more confident than others.]
- Now let's all play together as loudly and as happily as we can.
- [Signal to stop after a few minutes.].

Discussion

The following are useful prompts to encourage discussion:

- What was it like playing all together?
- Did it feel happy to you?
- Were there times when we were playing when it did not feel happy? Why?
- Were there times when you wanted to get up and dance?
- Did you start off feeling happy before we played?

- It is possible for music to change our emotions.
- Films and television programmes, and adverts, all use music to tell us how to feel. Can you think of examples of this?
- You can change how you feel by using music, either playing it or listening.
- Feeling happy is an important emotion.
- Although we only used percussion instruments, can you imagine what it is like using other instruments too?
- Everyone can play music to help how you feel. Not just those who learn to play an instrument.

Insecurity & Withdrawal

Young people can be crippled by feelings of insecurity and feel withdrawn when they experience loss. These emotions often come from a sense of being different, of not knowing who they are anymore, or from the very real experience of trauma that may result from a serious loss in their lives. As adolescents are already facing a significant stage of personal development, it is important to support these feelings of insecurity and withdrawal, so that the teenagers can continue developing into young adults with a healthy sense of identity, self-confidence and the ability to relate to others.

The exercises in this section are all aimed at supplying the necessary support and can be used with all young people who are struggling with these issues, as well as those who have experienced significant loss.

Activity 23

Insecurity & Withdrawal – Masks

Individual ✗   Group ✓

Materials

- Clear white masks that can be painted or decorated, enough for two per person
- Paints (preferably acrylic) and palettes
- Felt-tip pens
- Small craft materials for texture, such as feathers, stickers, shells, glitter, sand
- Brushes
- Fast-drying glue
- Background music (teacher's choice)
- The use of a mirror for young people to see themselves with their masks on

Aims and Overview

- Masks are a very ancient and useful tool that can help young people explore their sense of identity.

- In this exercise the group are going to make two masks to represent the different parts of themselves. One is the part they show the world, and one is the part that is their true and free self. This concept can help adolescents who are struggling to form their identity, as it helps them reflect on their character, and how they relate to others. It can help build up self-confidence for those who are feeling insecure, because the use of masks can allow a person the freedom to experiment. Young people can gain insights about how they feel just by making the masks.

- After making the masks, two levels of discussion are offered. The first is an opportunity for the young people to try on their own masks and to communicate with each other while wearing them. During the second they put the masks to one side and begin to reflect on their feelings about themselves.

- It is very important to offer both discussion opportunities, as masks are very potent and powerful. The second discussion provides young people with the opportunity to return to their everyday self, though perhaps with some new insights.

Preparation

- Ensure the activity takes place in a room suitable for art activities, where the young people can be messy and have space to make their own creations.
- Ensure that the atmosphere in the room is one of safety and relaxation. This can be achieved by playing music in the background, which can also help when teenagers need to concentrate on their mask-making.
- Lay out the materials attractively and provide each young person with two blank masks to start.

Instructions

Allow approximately 15 minutes for the making of each mask and guide the group through the exercise as follows:

- Sometimes when we have difficult experiences in life such as a loss, we can lose confidence, or we don't know how to face the world any more. When that happens it can be confusing.
- Today, to help with these feelings, you are going to make two masks each. One is to represent the face you show the world, and one to represent your free, true self. Does anyone have any questions? [Try to answer these first].
- Even if you have not had a difficult experience, mask-making can be fun and can help with gaining confidence.
- There is no right or wrong about what goes on the masks, you can make them as creatively as you want to. All the materials are here.
- First, think about the face you show the world. What might it look like? Look at the paints and craft materials, and then decide on the colours and textures you would like to use.
- When you are ready, come and get your materials and start making your first mask.
- When you have finished your first mask, think about your second mask, the free and true self. What might that look like? What materials would you use for this? Is it at all similar to the first mask? When you are ready, come and get the materials and make this mask. The first one will be drying.

◎ When you have finished both masks, tidy up your space and come and sit in a circle with them.

Discussion 1

The following are useful prompts to encourage discussion:

◎ This is your time to share what you have done and to try your masks on.

◎ If this is difficult, you can just show your masks to the group and say one thing about each mask.

◎ We will go around in a circle first, each saying something about our masks.

◎ Try and say something about why they are different, if you can. If you cannot say, just think about this.

◎ [Allow time for sharing the masks].

◎ Now that we have done that, does anyone want to try their masks on?

◎ Those who want to do so, can put their masks on now.

◎ Look around the room; do your friends look different? Do you feel different?

◎ For those wearing the masks, can you say something to the group, in turn, about who you are with the mask you are wearing? What does it make you feel? Try this with both masks. Which one do you prefer?

◎ Now take your masks off and shake off the feelings associated with them.

◎ Look around the group and recognise the people in your group without the masks. You are not your masks; they just express a part of you. But they may have helped you to understand how you feel about things in your life. We will talk more about this shortly.

◎ Decide what you want to do with your masks to keep them safe. They can be displayed on the wall if you would like this.

Discussion 2

Encourage the young people to return to their everyday selves, and to be more objective about the masks, by asking the following questions:

◎ How did they feel doing the exercise?

◎ Did they enjoy making the masks?

◎ Did they enjoy showing their masks?

- Did they enjoy trying the masks on and talking as the mask personality?
- What did the first mask make them think about?
- What did the second mask make them think about?
- What have they learnt about themselves and what they do and don't show the world about themselves?

The young people can also consider the following points:

- We all show different parts of ourselves to the world, at different times.
- The inner, free self does not often come out, but it is more likely to come out in adolescence.
- Wearing a mask can be very liberating, hence the popularity of masked balls and similar activities.

Activity 24

Insecurity & Withdrawal – Clay & Poetry

Individual ✗   Group ✓

Materials

- Air-drying clay for all members of the group
- Clay tools to make shapes, draw in clay, and similar
- Boards for working clay
- Display board for clay objects
- Aprons or old shirts for each young person
- Poems to read out loud
- Background music

Aims and Overview

- This exercise offers young people the chance to make shapes and explore how they feel through the medium of clay. This allows them a safe way to explore difficult feelings, which they can then discuss (if they wish) at the end of the activity.

- The use of materials such as clay allows young people to make something with their hands, which can often help when teenagers become withdrawn and insecure. It allows them to focus on something other than themselves, the making of an object, and to allow their feelings to be reflected in the art. They can 'project' their feelings onto the object, which can help them feel safer about expressing themselves publicly. This process of 'projection' has been described by some psychologists as the transference or projection of our unconscious thoughts or feelings onto a person or object (Grant & Crawley, 2002).

- Whilst they are making the clay shapes, the teenagers will hear one or two poems read out by the teacher to help inspire their creations. The poetry's themes are of withdrawal, hiding and insecurity.

- The reading of poetry while making an object allows young people both to forget their own feelings and thoughts, and also to reflect on what the poetry means. Two poems are suggested at the end of this exercise, but the teacher may choose others (see the suggested poets in Resources, 'Music, Poetry & Art Resources')

Preparation

Ensure that the young people can get messy by covering up their clothing with aprons or old shirts, and using a large, washable table. Also ensure that the mood in the room is safe and relaxed. Use music to help create this atmosphere if you can.

Instructions

Guide the group through the exercise as follows:

- Today we are going to make something from clay. This can be a recognisable shape, or a shape that just appears while you are working.
- This activity is related to the way that we sometimes feel withdrawn and lacking in confidence, how we sometimes hide ourselves, especially if we have experienced a loss.
- I will read a poem or two to you, while you are beginning to make the shapes.
- Take a lump of clay and find a place to sit at the desk with a board to work your clay in front of you.
- Begin by just getting to know the clay, smoothing it, touching it, pulling it apart, perhaps smelling it and thinking about whether you like it or not.
- See if a shape begins to appear.
- Then listen to the poetry while you are working with your shape. Think about what the poetry means and if you ever feel like this.
- [Read your poetry aloud.]
- You may find that an image comes into your head of a shape you want to make, while listening and thinking about the poems.
- But you don't have to make anything recognisable.
- Allow your hands to just make a shape, any shape.
- Try and trust that you will make the shape that is right for you.

- While you make the shape, allow it to change and develop as there is no right or wrong. Make sure you end up with a shape that reflects your experience of feeling withdrawn or less confident in some way.
- [Give the young people time to make their shape quietly.]
- When you are ready, place your shape on the display board.
- We will then discuss what you have done.

Discussion

Encourage the group to share both their clay shapes and their feelings as follows:

- Share your clay shape and describe it if you can.
- What does it mean for you?
- Was it hard or easy to make the final shape?
- Did hearing the poetry help this process?
- Are you surprised that others feel the same as you, if you often feel this way?
- If you feel withdrawn some of the time, did making the clay shape help?
- Choose what to do with your shapes at the end: you can display them, keep them, or store them at school.

Remember to offer extra support to any young person who is distressed as a result of this exercise.

Poetry Suggestions

Butterfly

I am like the butterfly
Flying, restless,
From flower to flower I move,
Searching, unsettled
I am hiding,
My light is shaded,
Hard to show others
Who I am
When I don't know myself?
My chrysalis gone, lost
My safety dissolved
I am exposed
To the elements,
To life.
I am like the butterfly
Landed on the rose
Smelling the nectar
Ready to jump
If wind and rain come
To lash at me.
I am delicate
A fragile, paper-thin
Shadow
Of who I will become
When I finally come to rest.
I am like the butterfly
Hidden and safe
Nestled in the crook
Of the purple flowers,
Camouflage comfort.
I am like the butterfly
Colours aglow
But you cannot see me
Yet.

Anna Jacobs

Harsh World

Outside is bleak
Inside is soft
Outside is sharp
Inside is soft
Outside is cruel
Inside is soft
Outside is a jungle
Inside is soft
But outside is the world
And inside I am hiding.

Anna Jacobs

Memories

Young people who have experienced grief and loss will need opportunities to explore their memories of the person they have lost. This is particularly true for those teenagers who are bereaved, as their need for memory stores will help as they develop into young adults. Sometimes young people are afraid that they will forget about the person they have lost, and other times they find it hard to remember as they feel the pain of their loss more severely when they do so. However, it is important for young people to recognise that their memories are important to them.

All the exercises in this section enable young people to think about and share some memories, and to make lasting memory stores that can help them as they move through a grieving process.

For those who have not had a significant loss, it can be useful to create memory stores simply as part of growing up.

Activity 25

Memories – 'I remember when ...'

Individual [X]   Group [✔]

> **Materials**
> - Whiteboard and markers
> - Pens and/or pencils and paper

Aims and Overview

- This exercise is about remembering incidents or details when someone important has been lost or another significant loss has been experienced. By allowing their memories to surface, young people can gain comfort, continue a healthy grieving process, and gain some support by sharing with others.

- Introduce this as an exercise in remembering. It is best done in a small group of up to ten young people. It can be hard to offer this activity to more than this number, as it is important to create some intimacy in the sharing part of the exercise.

- Young people will be asked in turn to complete the phrase, 'I remember when ...', at least twice.

- After the exercise they will have a discussion to support their responses to these answers.

Preparation

- Check that the venue for the group is suitable: comfortable and relaxed. Seat the group in a circle or around one table if possible, and be aware of vulnerable young people who may have had a recent loss. Provide extra staff for support, such as teaching assistants.

- Ensure that the time allotted for the session is sufficient, allowing at least half an hour for a group of approximately ten young people. In addition remember to check that the activity is before a break or lunch time if at school, so that the group members do not have to return immediately to normal classroom activities and subjects. They may need time to adjust after this exercise.

- This exercise can be used when only some members of a group have experienced loss, sometimes significant loss, or when all members have acknowledged some loss.

Instructions

- Begin by establishing a group contract and ground rules (see Resources, 'Sample Group Contract for Adolescents'). These help in providing a safe environment to encourage group members to be honest about their memories and feelings.
- Describe the exercise as above, reminding all the young people that they can choose any type of memory related to a loss they have experienced.
- Allow each young person time to complete the phrase, 'I remember when …', and encourage other members to listen in silence rather than instantly responding. Facilitate a discussion after each teenager has answered twice, using the prompts below.
- After this exercise they can continue to share their memories if they wish.
- Remind them that if they become upset at any point, there is extra support from other adults.

Discussion

The following are useful prompts to encourage discussion:

- What is it like to share your memories with your group?
- Has listening to other people's memories reminded you of more memories?
- Are some memories similar? Remember your memories are unique to you, even if they are similar to those of others.
- Did you find it hard or easy to think of memories? Do you know why?
- Have you ever written down or made something to do with your memories?
- Would you like to make a memory book or jar [Look at Activities 26 and 28 if the group expresses interest.]
- How often do you think about your memories?
- Does sharing them in this group help your feelings of loss?
- Do you know the phrase, 'Even though you have lost someone, you still have your memories'? Do you have any responses to this?
- Now that you have shared the memories in this group, are you able to offer each other support, if needed, at other times?

Activity 26

Memories – Memory Book

Individual ✔ Group ✔

Materials

- An exercise book or scrapbook for each young person
- Separate sheets of paper
- Felt-tip pens, crayons and other writing and art materials
- Photos brought in by members of the group
- Other small items brought in by the group (e.g., tickets to sports events, etc.)
- Craft materials
- Glue and brushes
- Worksheet 21, 'Memory Book', for each person

Aims and Overview

This exercise offers young people who have experienced a loss the chance to make a memory book for themselves. Adolescents and people who experience bereavement or another form of loss are often afraid that they will forget the person they have lost. By creating a memory book they can produce a lasting tribute to that person, which enables them to keep their memories in a safe place.

Preparation

- Ensure that the room in which the books will be made feels relaxed and safe for the group or an individual, as they will be considering memories that may evoke strong feelings.
- Ensure that the room is suitable for a small amount of artwork.
- A few days before the session ask the young people to bring in a photo or two of the person they have lost. They can also bring in small items such as tickets for football matches, which could be pasted into the book. Larger items are not suitable.
- Allow at least an hour to complete the activity.

Instructions

- Give an exercise book, a sheet of paper and Worksheet 21 to each young person doing this exercise.

- Ask them to read the worksheet briefly, and think about their own memories.

- Ask them to write a few memories down on the piece of paper. Give them about 10 minutes for this part of the exercise.

- When they have done this, ask them to choose the order in which they will place the memories in their book, and to decide what sort of materials they need, choosing from the writing, art and craft materials available. Instruct them to gather what they want together next to the place they are working.

- It is then time for them to write or draw and stick their memories into the book. There is no right or wrong way. Suggestions are on the worksheet.

- They can ask questions and ask for extra support at any time during the activity.

Activity 26

Worksheet 21

Memory Book

Here are some suggestions for things to put in your memory book and how to create it. However, there is no right or wrong way, and you can choose for yourself the order of pages.

- Page 1: Name of person you have lost and your relationship to them. What they looked like. Draw or write.

- Page 2: Memories of this person's character. Any examples you can remember, such as that they always hated rain, or they used to run 2 miles regularly.

- Page 3: Things this person did or said regularly.

- Page 4: Their favourite colour, football team, hobby, etc. Use any small items you have brought in.

- Page 5: A favourite holiday memory. You can draw, write or do crafts for this.

- Page 6: A funny memory; is there more than one?

- Page 7: A family memory; something you, as a family, like to think about.

- Page 8: A favourite memory of them from your own childhood. You may have been told a story by an adult, or you may remember something yourself.

- Page 9: Something you have been told about their childhood. You could ask your parent or another relative to help if you are not sure.

- Page 10: One sad memory, one happy memory, and one you will never forget.

When you have done enough, glue the photo on the front of the book to show who this book is in memory of.

It is your choice if you want to show anyone else this book. It is your memory book for you to keep, and you can add to it whenever you want. Take it home and keep it safe. It should help when you miss the person you have lost. Show your mum or dad, brothers or sisters, or another relative, so they know you have made it. They may have some more ideas of what to add.

Activity 27

Memories – Art Activity

Individual ☒   Group ✔

> **Materials**
> - A3 sheets of white cartridge paper
> - Squares of coloured card
> - Felt-tip pens, crayons
> - Glue and brushes
> - Whiteboard and markers

Aims and Overview

This exercise uses art and reflections to help young people to consider loss and how they may feel about any losses they have experienced or observed. Most young people have experienced some sort of loss.

Preparation

- Ensure the room is suitable for art activities.
- Introduce the exercise by asking the group to consider loss, and how they have felt when something even as simple as moving year at school has happened, or perhaps moving from primary to high school. Some will have experienced more loss than others, therefore be aware of the personal histories of the group members, if possible.
- Arrange for extra staff, such as teaching assistants, to be available if there are a number of vulnerable young people who have experienced significant loss in the group.
- Provide each young person with an A3 sheet of white paper.
- Write down the following words on the whiteboard: angry, sad, confused, lonely, happy, worried, frightened, anxious, intrigued, numb, surprised, appalled, shocked, withdrawn, dazed, relieved, empty, tired.

Page 1 of 2

Instructions

Guide the group through the exercise as follows:

- Think about a loss, either one you have experienced, or one you have read about or seen in a film or on television. If you wish you can imagine a loss. If you have experienced a significant loss recently, it is your choice if you wish to choose this loss.
- Choose a coloured card to represent this loss. It can be any colour, let your instincts guide you.
- Now glue this card in the centre of the white paper. This represents your loss.
- Looking at the whiteboard, can you think of a number of feeling words associated with this loss? You may think of other words too.
- Write your choice of feeling words around the coloured card that represents the loss, using different colours.
- The words can be small or large, or placed near or far from the card. You can choose as few or as many as you like.
- You can write what the loss is in the centre of the coloured card if you want to.
- When you are ready, try and join in the discussion about your loss artwork.

Discussion

The following are useful prompts to encourage discussion:

- Did your emotions feel strong or weak during this art-making exercise?
- Were you surprised at the words on the board?
- Did you use your own words?
- Does your artwork express some of what you feel at your loss?
- Does your artwork help with the feelings?
- Is it OK to tell others how you feel?
- Do some of your group feel similarly? This would not be surprising, as most people who experience loss have some feelings in common.
- Is there one thing you can add to your artwork to help with these feelings?
- If you would like to keep this artwork, perhaps you can add to it over time and find out if your feelings change.
- If your feelings are very strong, tell someone after this exercise so that we can support you.

Activity 28

Memories – Memory Bowl

Individual ✔   Group ✔

Materials

- Aprons or old shirts to cover clothing
- Music for relaxation
- Paper and pens
- Air-hardening clay
- Tools for making clay items
- Boards for working clay
- Acrylic paints
- Palettes and paintbrushes

Aims and Overview

- This exercise offers young people the chance to make a clay bowl, and to put several small items into it that represent some of their memories of loss. It can be very therapeutic to work with clay when considering loss and memories. By making a memory bowl, young people can keep their memories and return to this bowl whenever they need extra comfort and support.

- The activity is suitable for any young person who has experienced a loss. It can be used for a whole class or in a smaller group specifically supporting grief and loss.

- Allow the young people to share and talk while they are making their clay bowls and objects. This can become an informal sharing of their loss, and can be as helpful as the creative process of making the objects.

Page 1 of 3

Preparation

- Ensure that the environment is relaxed and safe enough for young people to think about their losses and their memories. If there are young people in the group who have experienced significant loss, provide extra support, such as from teaching assistants.
- Ensure that the young people can get messy by covering up their clothing with aprons or old shirts, and using a large, washable table.
- Provide music to create a more relaxing environment.
- This activity takes place on two separate occasions, as the young people will need to wait for their clay objects to dry after session 1, before painting them in session 2.

Instructions: Session 1

Provide each person with a piece of paper, a lump of clay, access to the tools, and a board to work on. Guide the group through the exercise as follows:

- Think about a loss you have experienced that holds some memories for you. If it is a significant loss, remember there is extra support, if needed, from other adults.
- When you are ready, write down about four or five memories. Each of these memories is going to be represented by a small shape held within the clay bowl that you will also make.
- For example, a mini-leaf or flower could be used for experiences in nature, a hammer or football for experiences in a workshop or football match. Think about your own memories and decide what shapes you would like. There is no right or wrong.
- You don't have to be great artists to make your shapes, just find something that has meaning for you.
- Think about the shape and colour for each memory, and note this down on your piece of paper.
- When you are ready, use the clay to form your memory shapes.
- Remember that when you are finished, the shapes are all going to be placed in one bowl, so they cannot be too large.
- When you have finished, put them carefully to one side to dry; you will paint them in the second session.
- Now use a larger piece of clay to make your bowl. Look at the shapes you have made and make sure the size will hold them.
- Choose the shape of your bowl. It can be tall, square, round, oblong or even a box if you prefer.

- Ask for help if you are not sure how to do this.
- When you are finished, place your bowl carefully on the board so it can dry.
- Keep your piece of paper so that you will know how to decorate the symbols in the second session.

Choose a safe place to store all the clay while it is drying, ready to be painted in session 2.

Instructions: Session 2

Make sure everyone has their own bowl and memory shapes and provide each young person with a palette, brushes and access to the paints. Guide the group through the exercise as follows:

- Now that your clay bowls and objects have dried, it is time to paint them.
- Do you remember your memories? Check your piece of paper from the first session if you have forgotten.
- Choose your colours and, using the palettes and brushes, paint your memory shapes.
- Once they are dry, you can take these home and use them whenever you need to think about your memories.

Relaxation

It is very important for young people to be able to relax at times, when they have experienced a loss. Sometimes this is because they are not sleeping well, due to their grief, or because they cannot concentrate in class, or it can be due to feeling stressed, anxious or worried as a result of their loss. Relaxation techniques vary, and include music, massage (at home, not at school), the use of essential oils, reading a good book, going for a walk or taking other exercise, such as yoga (see Resources, 'Resources for Stress Relief'). Young people do not normally focus on relaxation, because they are usually too busy having fun, doing schoolwork and growing up. Therefore this exercise can be used when young people are seen to need relaxation as part of their experience of loss.

Activity 29

Relaxation Exercise

Individual ✔   Group ✔

Aims and Overview

This exercise is to help young people relax. It offers a guided visualisation and a way for them to feel calmer. It can be used in a variety of situations to help when young people have experienced loss. It can also be used as a general calming exercise.

Preparation

- Ensure the room is a comfortable and relaxed room, preferably with a carpet where the young people can lie down to relax fully. Alternatively they can sit in their chairs and relax.
- Calming music can be used to enhance the effect of the visualisation exercise, if you wish.
- At first it may seem strange to the young people to do this sort of exercise, but if they persist most will find it extremely helpful. It may be useful to remind them that many people, such as sportsmen and women, use guided visualisation to build up their sense of wellbeing and ability to win.

Instructions

When you are ready to read out the instructions, take your time and read each one slowly and clearly. Allow a few moments between each instruction. At the end of the exercise, ask the young people if they do feel more relaxed. Ask the group to do the following:

- Find a place in the room where you can lie down or sit quietly and begin to relax.
- I am going to guide you on an inner journey to help you become calmer, so it is important that your body is relaxed when we start.
- Scan your body, and if you find there are places where you feel tense, allow them to relax by doing a quick shake and tense-up, followed by allowing yourself to become floppy.
- Take a few deep breaths and, on each out breath, feel your body becoming more heavy and relaxed.

- Allow one more deep breath, seeking out any remaining tension.
- Now imagine you are in a beautiful, peaceful and restful place outdoors.
- It may be a garden, a meadow, a wood or somewhere else.
- The sun is warm on your body, there is a gentle breeze and all is well.
- Can you smell the greenery, hear the birds singing tunefully, feel the ground underneath you?
- Don't worry if you can't see it; just imagine how it would feel.
- It is a good place and no harm will come to you here.
- Within this place, there are some special sites of water.
- Look for the water: it could be a running stream or a fountain.
- When you have found it, imagine yourself moving towards it.
- When you are near it, can you see a way to touch the water safely?
- The water will be clear, pure and flowing.
- If you can, either imagine yourself washing with the water, or drink from it if there is a cup nearby. Both are fine.
- This water is there to help wash away any tensions, so you can return relaxed.
- Finally, imagine that nearby there is a large, old, solid oak tree.
- Sit by it so your spine is against the tree.
- Allow the tree to fill you with life: feel its sap rising and, with it, your body becoming filled with energy.
- Feel its roots deep in the earth, and let your body feel it has roots too.
- Imagine the sun on its branches, bringing it to life with green leaves and acorns.
- Allow the oak to pour some of its strength into you, as you prepare to return to your day.
- Then, when you are ready, slowly come back to the room, first feeling your body on the floor or in your chair, and then open your eyes. Make sure you are fully back in the room.
- Do you feel more relaxed, yet energised?
- Some people find this sort of exercise easier than others to do. Don't worry, you will all have benefited in some way.
- Try and keep this feeling for the rest of the day.

On Death & Dying

Young people who experience the bereavement of a close family member or friend are often shocked at their reactions. They also, however, often have questions that they find hard to ask. They may never have experienced the death of someone close before, and it will have brought up many issues related to life and what happens afterwards. These can be spiritual in emphasis, but also practical, depending on the nature of the death.

For example, a death from an illness can cause many questions about whether or not the person was in pain before death, and even how important it was for them to choose to be buried or cremated. Other deaths, for example death in an accident or sudden death by heart attack, bring with them the question of whether these things could have been avoided. Finally, the most difficult form of death for young people to cope with is a violent death, either by murder or suicide. Questions and thoughts about this type of death can be extremely hard for young people to ask or handle, particularly since the rest of the family is often too close to the experience to be available. Therefore, it can be extremely helpful for young people to have another place to go to ask questions, consider their beliefs and explore the meaning of death.

The exercises in this section give all young people the opportunity to ask questions and offer some specific outlets for those who have experienced the death of someone close.

Activity 30

Death & Dying – How do You Feel About Death?

Individual ☒   Group ☑

Aims and Overview

- This exercise helps a group of teenagers to discuss death in a general, rather than a specific, sense. Those who have experienced a very recent bereavement should be given the opportunity to join in, because such a discussion can be very helpful in enabling support from peers, developing empathy and preparing for any future losses.

- Remember that most young people will have experienced death in the media, in films, in books, in computer games and in the news. They will all have encountered death in one way or another. They may also often have watched programmes on television portraying brutal death or fantasy deaths, in which those who die return to life. All of these aspects of death can be discussed.

Preparation

- This exercise is a discussion around death and dying. Ensure that any adults facilitating the discussion are comfortable with the language of death, as many professionals do have some issues with using words such as 'dying' or 'death'. Also ensure that none of the adults have had a recent or complex experience of grief and loss, which could affect them during this discussion.

- Ensure that you are aware of any members of the group who have a history of bereavement before doing this exercise.

- Inform families and young people prior to this exercise that you will be discussing issues related to death and dying. This enables families to both prepare young people and to inform you of any losses that have occurred that you may not know of. Death is an emotive subject for both adults and young people, but young people can often be more affected than we realise. Therefore you should try to be as prepared as possible.

- Examine the guidelines on how to facilitate a group at the beginning of this chapter, so that you have the skills to support this discussion.

Page 1 of 2

Instructions and Discussion

Introduce the topic of death and dying as a general topic for discussion, using the prompts below to encourage an exchange of ideas. Remember to offer extra support or someone to talk to if any of these questions upset a young person. Death and dying are difficult subjects, particularly for those who have experienced loss.

The following are useful prompts to encourage discussion:

- Have you ever thought about death before? Why, or why not? How do you feel talking about death and dying?
- Does anyone want to share any personal experiences of death, perhaps the death of a pet or relative?
- Could each person in the group give one example of something to do with death that they have experienced or wondered about?
- What do you think happens at death?
- Do you know what various faiths think about what happens at death?
- Have you ever seen a dead animal, for example, on the road? Did this affect you at all?
- Have you listened to the news and heard reports of someone dying, for example, soldiers involved in a war? Did this affect you at all?
- What do you think you need to know about death at your age? For example, do you need to decide where you wish to be buried?
- Do you know what a will is? Do you know if anyone in your family has made a will? What would you put in your own will?
- Have you ever been to a funeral? Do you know what happens at a funeral?
- What do you think about burial or cremation? Would you prefer one or the other for a family member or yourself?
- Does your family have a particular faith? Does this mean you have a traditional practice when someone in your family dies?
- Did you know some philosophers believe that if we wake up preparing for the day as if it was our last day, we can live life more fully? What do you think of this?
- What would you like to think happens at death?
- Do you believe in God? Is this important when thinking about death?
- Are there other important things you want to know about death?
- To finish this discussion, try to decide as a group on some sentences that are important for you all concerning death and dying.

Activity 31

Death & Dying – Questions about a Bereavement

Individual ✔   Group ✔

Materials

- Worksheet 22, 'My Experience of Loss'

Aims and Overview

This exercise offers those who have experienced bereavement the opportunity to think about their experiences of death and what death means to them now as a result. It then offers them the chance to share ideas and thoughts with others who have had a similar experience. This is very supportive for most young people.

Preparation

- This exercise is only for those who have experienced a significant bereavement. It can take place in a bereavement agency, or at school if there are enough young people (although no more than six or seven) who have had an experience of loss.

- It is possible to use this exercise with individuals, if they have someone (a counsellor or someone else) with whom to discuss their answers.

- If undertaken in a group setting, ensure that each young person involved in the activity is happy talking to the others.

- Ensure that the young people wish to talk about some aspects of their bereavement, and that the stage of grief they are at allows them to be comfortable talking. Some young people will want to explore these topics very early in their grief and others will want to wait until their very raw feelings have lessened.

- Ensure that the person leading this exercise is happy to use the language of death and dying, and is able to tolerate and support strong feelings of grief if they emerge. It is helpful to have at least one other support adult nearby, a teaching assistant, or similar.

Page 1 of 2

- Ensure that the environment is relaxed and safe enough for the teenagers to talk about difficult thoughts and feelings together. Create a relaxing atmosphere by playing music, allowing them to sit on the floor or to take off their shoes, and so on.

- Prepare the young people in advance by telling them that they will work with a worksheet asking them questions related to their bereavement, and that this might bring up difficult memories and feelings. They can choose to leave some questions unanswered or to leave the group if they feel they need to.

Instructions and Discussion

- Each young person is given a copy of Worksheet 22, which asks them pertinent questions about their loss and experience of bereavement. Allow at least twenty minutes for them to complete the questionnaire.

- They are then brought together as a group, to discuss their answers.

- Facilitate the discussion by working through the questions and answers on the worksheet.

- These are sensitive questions, therefore the teacher leading this discussion will need extra support for any of the young people who become upset. They will also need to be sensitive in their facilitation (see the guidelines for facilitators at the beginning of this chapter).

- At the end of the discussion, the young people may choose to meet again, as teenagers often find it supportive to meet with others who have had a similar experience of bereavement, even if the cause and the person they have lost is different. Choose whether to arrange a second meeting for them.

Activity 31

Worksheet 22

My Experience of Loss

This exercise is to help you think about some of the experiences of loss you have had recently. It may be distressing at times to answer the questions, but it may also be helpful for you to understand and ask yourself the questions. You could find it valuable to think again about some of the deeper questions that came up for you at that time, and to consider what death now means for you as a result of your loss. Answer each question as honestly as you can, and remember that at any time you can ask for support if you get upset.

These questions are about the person in your life who died. If you are not happy answering them, it may be too soon for you to think about doing this exercise. But try if you want to.

1 What was the cause of death? And how long ago did this happen?

_____

_____

_____

2 Do you ever talk about the experience of losing someone? Who to? Do you think about it often?

_____

_____

_____

3 If the death was from an illness such as cancer or similar, did you know that they were going to die? How did you know? Did this help when the time came?

_____

_____

_____

4 Can you remember how you felt when you were told that they had died? Did you believe it?

_____

_____

_____

5 Did you ever think about death before this happened?

_____

_____

_____

6 What did you believe about death, if anything? Such as, there is nothing after death, there is life after death, God looks after you, and so on.

_____

_____

_____

7 Has what you believe now changed? If it has changed, say how?

_____

_____

_____

8 If your loss was from a sudden or violent death, are you left with questions you would have liked to ask? What are they? Who would you like to ask?

_____
_____
_____

9 If your loss was from an illness and there was some time before the death, are you still left with questions you would have liked to ask?

_____
_____
_____

10 Did you go to the funeral? If you did, what was it like? If not, what was that like? Did you have any involvement in the funeral?

_____
_____
_____

11 Did you have any faith, such as in God, before your loved one died? Did this change after the death? If you did not have a faith, has that changed and do you now have a faith?

_____
_____
_____

12 What do you think happens at death?

_____

_____

_____

13 Has having this experience made you think more about your own or other people's death? Has it made you think of other things, such as how you live your life, now that you have been bereaved? How has it changed you? If it has.

_____

_____

_____

14 Do you ever have a sense of the person who died being near you? Or do you visit the grave and feel this? If you do not visit the grave, or memorial place, would you like to?

_____

_____

_____

15 Are you able to speak to your family about any of these things? If not, would you like to?

_____

_____

_____

16 Is there a question you would like to ask about your experience?

_____

_____

_____

17 What, if anything, helps when you think about these things now? Are you able to do normal things like go out, have fun, do your work?

_____

_____

_____

After you have answered these questions, we are going to speak as a group about your answers. Each person in your group has had a bereavement, so you all have that in common. It can be supportive to speak about these things with others who have had similar experiences. Your teacher will support this conversation. You can also decide if you want to meet more than once.

Chapter 6
Resources

A Sample School Bereavement Policy	212
Template for a Letter to a Family Following Bereavement	214
Template for a Time-Out Card	215
Sample Group Contract for Adolescents	216
Plan for a General Assembly on Bereavement	217
Information on Anti-Bullying Policies	219
Further Reading	221
Useful Websites	223
Music, Poetry & Art Resources	225

A Sample School Bereavement Policy

- Establish contact with the family (either by phone, letter or home visit) when a young person experiences bereavement due to any significant cause.

- Establish who in the school the family wishes to be informed about the bereavement. Sometimes this is just the head or subject teacher, but it could be the entire staff, the young person's friends, their whole class or even everyone in the school.

- Find out what the young person has been told as soon as possible, so that others can support them and avoid telling them something they do not already know. This is particularly important for losses such as suicide: sometimes families choose not to give all the details immediately to young people, even those in their late teens.

- Offer support from a key person in the school. This can be a person who already has responsibility for bereavement support, or someone specific to this young person and family. This person should not be someone who has had a recent bereavement themselves.

- Give guidance as to whether a young person should return to school, have work sent home to them, or put aside all work for a set time. This will depend on the young person's reaction to the loss, the family's wishes and the stage of schooling of the adolescent. Many young people prefer life to remain as normal as possible immediately after a loss and to see their friends. Others find it impossible to be normal as they are too upset, although they may attempt to hide it.

- Offer a time-out card once a young person returns to school: this allows them to leave a classroom without asking permission, should they feel the need. Remember to describe how to use it when it is offered.

- Give a young person choices in the first few weeks: specifically, name the person to whom they may go if they need to leave class when they are upset or lose concentration.

- Ensure there is support for the young person if they wish this; do this discretely, for example, checking if they want close friends nearby, want to be quiet at breaks, or if they would like to speak to someone such as a counsellor.

- Provide support at the time of the funeral, from a distance if necessary, by offering to send a teacher to the funeral if the family would like that, and by sending a card. Many families appreciate this gesture, especially if the school is an important base in the community.

- Do not avoid talking about death and loss; allow this as a possible conversation with the bereaved young people and others, if needed.

- Remember that the pain from loss does not simply stop after a few months. Create a list of anniversaries the young person will have to face: birthdays, date of death, Christmas, Mother's and Father's Day. The list can become a file that will follow the young person through their life at the school. Monitor, in particular, when the young person changes stages in education, and keep new teachers informed of their circumstances.

- Monitor if the young person shows particular distress or changes of attitude or behaviour over a period of time, and offer extra support if needed.

- Keep in touch with the family during the first few months in particular. Check if significant changes occur in the family life as a result of the loss. If the bereavement was a particularly shocking or sudden loss, issues of grief may not occur for a few months.

- Monitor the impact of more than one bereavement in a class or school community. If necessary, offer a whole school assembly on bereavement and loss.

- Keep a list of local and national resources for guidance, extra support and information.

Template for a Letter to a Family Following Bereavement

Dear _____

We were very sorry to hear of your recent loss. We are writing to express our support as a community for you and your family, and to ask if there is anything we can offer in the way of particular support at this time.

When a young person in our care experiences a bereavement, we usually like to support you in a way that suits your circumstances. If you could, do let us know how we can do this, including what [name of young person] understands has happened, and how he/she has been involved in the loss, so that we can support him/her at this most difficult time. We will take our guidance from you as to how to tell the class, his/her friends and the school community.

We can choose a key person within the school for [name of young person] to go to whenever he/she needs extra support while in school, as well as giving him/her a 'time-out' card that he/she can use whenever he/she feels they need to leave lessons. We will inform all of our staff who come into contact with [name of young person] of the circumstances, so that they can support him/her as needed.

Please feel you can ring us at any point if you would like to talk through any particular needs you believe [name of person] may have at this time. He/she may be very upset, or tired, and may also need a few days off school. Please be assured that this is normal. We can provide schoolwork if needed. [name of young person] may, however, also wish to return to school and see his/her friends, to be reminded of other things and forget his/her loss. We will support whatever decisions you may make regarding attendance at school at this time, and will offer extra support in school if [name of young person's] wish is to return immediately.

With our sincerest condolences,

[Name of head teacher/person signing on behalf of the school]

Template for a Time-Out Card

Time-Out Card for _____   Date _____

This card is to give permission for _____ to leave lessons whenever he/she needs to do so, without permission.

He/she will go to _____ [give specific name of room/reception] or meet _____ [name of member of staff].

If _____ is very upset, he/she is allowed to take a close friend with her/him.

_____ has promised to use this card only when needed, but there is no limit to the number of times it can be used.

It will be reviewed weekly.

_____

[Signature of head teacher/class teacher]

Sample Group Contract for Adolescents

*If possible, enable the adolescents in choosing
their own ground rules for how to behave during a group.
These are some suggestions:*

- **Confidentiality:** We will keep everything we say to each other about personal matters confidential.

- **Listening:** We will listen carefully and not interrupt.

- **Respect:** We will take turns to say something and be respectful when someone is speaking. We will ask any questions respectfully.

- **Boundaries:** We will keep to any time limits agreed for the group and will not resort to physical violence at any point.

- **Sensitivity to feelings:** We will be sensitive to the feelings shown by others in the group.

- **Contribution:** We will all attempt to contribute to the group discussion as openly as possible. However it is OK not to contribute if you do not wish to.

- **Non-judgemental approach:** If we comment on something someone else has done, we will not be rude or aggressive, even if we disagree.

Plan for a General Assembly on Bereavement

- Open the meeting with a piece of beautiful but sombre music (Bach, for example) as everyone enters the hall.

- The school might also set up a screen behind the main platform, showing images such as death from war or natural disaster. This should be fairly low-key and unobtrusive.

- Begin with a brief talk about death and dying. A suggested opening line might be: 'We hope that someone close to us never dies, but sometimes this happens. We are going to think about this and talk about what happens, and how families say goodbye.'

- If the person who has recently lost someone close has given permission, it is possible to add: 'We are also going to think of [name of bereaved student] who recently lost a family member.

- Describe the rituals surrounding death in different religions and parts of the world, from the UK to examples such as the Mexican Day of the Dead. Do not forget to mention what happens in this country, but remind the young people that families all over the world mourn and grieve for their loved ones just as we do. We are all the same.

- If you wish, refer to Christian beliefs and customs, but remember that there are many customs now in this country.

- Talk about the typical role of funerals and memorials, also the fact that there are many types of ceremony in today's Britain. See the Dying Matters website ('Resources: Useful Websites') for literature discussing this subject.

- Remind the young people that although we hope never to experience serious loss while we are young, young people around the world do experience tragic loss on a daily basis sometimes, and it is important to remember them.

- Mention some of the different things that can cause loss and bereavement: illness, accidents, military service, suicide, wars and tragic natural disasters.

- Particular mention can be made here of military conflicts and wars that cause huge loss, as well as organisations such as the UN and the Red Cross, both of which attempt to keep peace and offer healing and medical facilities for those around the world facing loss through armed conflicts.

- Talk about the feelings that young people have to face when they lose someone they love: sadness, anger, fear, upset, worry and anxiety.

- Continue by saying that death and loss are always part of a person's life, but that these are not things to be afraid of. We cannot change the fact that death happens, or that we may have loss from another cause, but we can change how we respond to it, with support and information.

- If the school has contact with a local hospice, remind the students that it is often possible to arrange a visit if they are at all interested in how the health and charity sector support the dying. (Many hospices have open days or invite schools to visit to help educate young people on the work of a hospice.)

- Keep a minute's silence or play a piece of music to show respect both for anyone in the school who has lost a loved one and all of children and young people around the world who have lost someone important.

- Finish by saying that if anyone is particularly upset as a result of this assembly, they can speak to a teacher or teaching assistant afterwards.

- As the young people leave the hall, try to arrange that a good piece of music is played to wordlessly acknowledge the feelings and impressions connected to death.

Information on Anti-Bullying Policies

Various resources exist to support schools when devising an anti-bullying policy, which is now necessary in law. The websites http://www.bullying.co.uk and http://www.kidscape.org.uk are both full of resources for devising effective anti-bullying strategies. Kidscape has a downloadable anti-bullying policy that covers topics such as: 'What is Bullying?'; 'Why is it Important to Respond?'; 'Policy Objectives'; 'Signs and Symptoms'; and 'Procedures: Outcomes'.

The NSPCC and Childline also offer comprehensive resources for anti-bullying practices, including the 'NSPCC School, Academy and College Anti-Bullying Policy Checklist'. Below are two sections taken from this checklist (see http://www.nspcc.org.uk/Inform):

Prevention: detailing what the school does to stop bullying taking place

- Provides key messages to promote respectful relationships and positive behaviour.
- Promotes positive behaviour, and refers to the appropriate school's Rules/Code of Conduct
- Helps pupils to understand what constitutes bullying in its different forms, its impact and the roles of those involved in bullying behaviour including bystanders
- Helps to develop the personal, social and emotional skills that help protect pupils from bullying.
- Addresses online safety with its pupils and parents/carers
- Provides supervision between lessons, at breaks and lunchtimes
- Provides safe places for vulnerable groups at breaks and lunchtimes
- Recognises and celebrates diversity
- Has activities and events, including Anti-Bullying Week, that address bullying

Intervention: what the school does when bullying takes place

- Identifies the procedures for pupils and parents/carers reporting bullying incidents
- Acknowledges that the school will respond to bullying involving its pupils whether it has taken place in or outside of school
- Identifies the strategies the school uses to respond to bullying incidents to protect and support those being bullied

- Identifies the strategies the school uses to engage those who have bullied to acknowledge their responsibility, to recognize the harm caused and to support them to change their behaviour
- References how bullying incidents are recorded, and how those records are monitored
- Provides details of how the school works with external agencies to address bullying behaviour
- Details how the school will engage with parents/carers
- Details how parents can express concerns and make a formal complaint when they feel the school has not acted appropriately to address bullying
- Identifies how the school assesses the severity of the bullying and the range of disciplinary sanctions it can impose, describes what the school expects of those who are bystanders and how the school will react where pupils fail to respond to protect those who are being bullied.

Further Reading

Heegaard M., 1988, *When Someone Very Special Dies*, Woodland Press, New York.

> A very well-established workbook that can be used by younger adolescents to explore their own experience of loss.

Heegaard M., 1988, *When Something Terrible Happens*, Woodland Press, New York.

> A workbook for non-specific but traumatic loss, similar to the workbook above.

Jacobs, A., 2014, *Rory's Story: a Teenager's Story of Loss*, Hinton House Publishers, Buckingham.

> A therapeutic story for teenagers that introduces many aspects of loss in a gritty, readable tale.

Ness P., 2011, *A Monster Calls*, Candlewick Press, Somerville MA.

> A 'haunting and darkly funny novel' aimed at older teenagers. The book follows Conor as he faces the illness of his mother with the help of the 'monster' who is both terrifying and dreamlike. It is a captivating and rewarding read for all who have faced, or are facing, the loss of a close relative.

Pitcher A., 2011, *My Sister Lives on the Mantlepiece*, Orion, London.

> A 10-year-old boy reflects on his family life after the death, five years previously, of his sister in a terrorist bomb attack. Suitable for young teenagers

Rosen M., 2011, *Michael Rosen's Sad Book*, Walker Books, London.

> A book (fantastically illustrated by Quentin Blake) that reflects the sadness we all feel when we experience loss; written in memory of Michael Rosen's son.

White E.B., 2003, *Charlotte's Web*, Puffin, London.

> This classic is the tale of a spider who befriends a pig. The author uses their friendship with each other and a little girl to touch on many important themes of life, including loss and love.

Wilson J., 2001 *Vicky Angel*, Corgi Yearling, London.

> The story of a young girl coming to terms with the loss of her best friend, who decides to remain as an angel in her life. Themes of grief and guilt are combined with an excellent story of how a young girl reshapes her life beyond loss. Excellent for mid to older teens.

Further Reading

Resources for Stress Relief

Bodhipaksa, 2012, *Mindfulness Meditations for Teens*, Wildmind, Newmarket NH. Audio CD

Chryssicas M.K., 2007, *Breathe*, Dorling Kindersley, London. Book and DVD

Purperhart H. & Van Amelsfort B., 2009, *Yoga Exercises for Teens*, Hunter House Publishers Inc, Alameda CA. An accessible book for teenagers.

http://www.smilingmind.com Smiling Mind is an online resource (also an Australian charity) for teenagers. It offers 'modern meditation for young people' based on sound research into mindfulness techniques.

Useful Websites

http://www.winstonswish.org.uk

> Winston's Wish, the Gloucester-based charity, has an interactive website for children to use, as well as resources such as books and memory boxes for sale. It has a helpline, an online resource to support school professionals and a comprehensive list of books for bereaved children.

http://www.childbereavement.org.uk

> Child Bereavement is one of the main UK bereavement organisations supporting bereaved children, young people, parents and professionals. It offers training courses, individual support, group support and some resources.

http://www.childhoodbereavementnetwork.org.uk

> The foremost charity supporting bereaved children and young people in the UK. It is involved in policy-making, holds a list of all bereavement services for young people in the UK, and offers resources for teenagers (such as cards to be given to a young person when they are bereaved).

http://www.crusebereavementcare.org.uk

> National charity supporting bereaved adults, children and young people. It provides details of services for children and young people and offers bereavement support to young people in some areas of the UK. It offers RD 4U, a website specifically for young people, and a brochure, 'After Someone Dies' is available from them.

http://www.dyingmatters.org

> A government-led initiative that offers some excellent resources for families to approach conversations about death and dying.

http://www.baat.org

> British Association of Art Therapists, to which all art psychotherapists belong, and which regulates practice, offers training and monitors standards.

http://www.bapt.info

> British Association of Play Therapists, a professional organisation promoting Play Therapy for enhancing the mental health and emotional well-being of children and young people.

Useful Websites

http://www.un.org/en

> The United Nations is an international organisation founded in 1945 after the Second World War by 51 countries. It is committed to maintaining international peace and security, developing friendly relations among nations and promoting social progress, better living standards and human rights.

http://www.redcross.org.uk

> A volunteer-led humanitarian organisation that helps people in crisis, whoever and wherever they are.

http://www.muchloved.com

> An online memorial charity helping bereaved people to create their own personalised and free online memorial in memory of a loved one.

http://www.gonetoosoon.org

> A free online memorial site to create a lasting tribute to a relative or friend.

Music, Poetry & Art Resources

Music: Sadness

Beethoven, *Moonlight Sonata*

Bruce Springsteen, 'The River'

Chopin, *Funeral March*

Dire Straits, 'Brothers in Arms'

Leonard Cohen, 'Suzanne'

Simon and Garfunkel, 'The Sound of Silence'

Mozart, *Requiem Mass in D Minor*

Music: Anger

Holst, *The Planets*, 'Jupiter'

Pink Floyd, 'The Wall'

Red Hot Chili Peppers, 'Around the World'

Most 'heavy metal' band music

Drum music

Music: Relaxation

J.S. Bach, most music

Ludovico Einaudi, all of his music

Dolphin or whale sounds

Native American flute music

Poetry: Sadness

Lord Byron

Sylvia Plath

W.B. Yeats

William Shakespeare

Visual Art: Sadness

Edward Degas, 'The Absinthe Drinker'

Käthe Kollwitz, most of her images are of very sad people

Picasso, 'The Old Guitarist' and other art from his Blue Period

Rembrandt, 'Jeremiah Lamenting the Destruction of Jerusalem'

Vincent Van Gogh, most of his later work

On-line purchase of arts and crafts materials for use in the public sector

YPO (http://www.ypo.co.uk)

The Consortium (http://www.educationsupplies.co.uk)

Hope Education (http://www.hope-education.co.uk)

References & Bibliography

Argyle M., 2001, *The Psychology of Happiness*, Routledge, London.

Astley N., 2003, *Do Not Go Gentle*, Bloodaxe Books, Northumberland.

Bee H., 1995, *The Growing Child*, Harper Collins, New York.

Biswas-Diener R. & Kashdan T.B., 2013, 'What Happy People Do Differently', *Psychology Today 7*, pp50–59.

Bloom W., 2001, *The Endorphin Effect*, Piatkus, London.

Bowlby J., 1969, *Attachment and Loss*, vol. 1, Hogarth Press, London.

Burnett F. H., 1975, *The Secret Garden*, Dent & Sons, Surrey.

Case C. & Dalley T. (eds), 2007, *Art Therapy with Children: from Infancy to Adolescence*, Routledge, London.

Clews V. & Rowe A., 2010, *Relaxation Techniques for a Healthy Life*, Natural Harmony Productions, Andover. Audio CD.

Crittenden P.M., 2008, *Raising Parents: Attachment Parenting and Child Safety*, Routledge, New York.

Crittenden P.M. & Landini A., 2011, *Assessing Adult Attachment*, Norton & Company, New York.

Dyregrov A., 1991, *Grief in Children: a Handbook for Adults*, Jessica Kingsley, London.

Erikson E., 1950, *Childhood and Society*, Norton, New York.

Gibran K., 1926, *The Prophet*, William Heinemann, London.

Grant J. & Crawley J., 2002, *Transference and Projection: Mirrors to the Self*, Open University Press, Buckingham.

Gibson J. (ed.), 2001, *Thomas Hardy: The Complete Poems*, Macmillan, London.

Harrison L. & Harrington R., 2001, 'Adolescents' Bereavement Experiences: Prevalence, Association with Depressive Symptoms, and Use of Services', *Journal of Adolescence* 24, pp159–69.

Harter S., 1987, 'The determinations and mediational role of global self-worth in Children', N. Eisenberg (ed.) *Contemporary Topics in Developmental Psychology*, Wiley-Interscience, New York.

Harter S., 1990, 'Processes underlying Adolescent Self-concept Formation', R. Montemayor, G.R. Adams, & T.P. Gullota (eds) *From Childhood to Adolescence: A Transitional Period*, Sage, Newbury Park.

Holmes J., 1993, *John Bowlby & Attachment Theory*, Routledge, London.

Jacobs A., 2013, *Supporting Children through Grief & Loss*, Hinton House Publishers, Buckingham.

Jacobs A., 2014, *Rory's Story: a Teenager's Story of Loss*, Hinton House Publishers, Buckingham.

Jennings S., 2011, *101 Activities for Empathy & Awareness*, Hinton House Publishers, Buckingham.

Jennings S., 2013a, *Creative Activities for Developing Emotional Intelligence*, Hinton House Publishers, Buckingham

Jennings S., 2013b, *101 Activities for Social & Emotional Resilience*, Hinton House Publishers, Buckingham.

Kasket E., 2012, 'Continuing Bonds in the Age of Social Networking: Facebook as a Modern Day Medium', *Bereavement Care*, 31(2), pp62–69.

Klass D. et al. (eds), 1996, *Continuing Bonds*, Taylor & Francis, Washington DC.

Kübler-Ross E., 1969, *On Death and Dying*, Touchstone, New York.

Leary T., 1972, *Psychedelic Prayers*, Academy Editions, London.

Luvmor J. & Luvmor S., 2007, *Everyone Wins! Co-operative Games and Activities*, New Society Publishing, Canada.

Muir A., 2010, *Relaxation Techniques: Teach Yourself*, Hodder, London.

Neimeyer R.A., 2001, 'The Language of Loss', R.A. Neimeyer (ed.), *Meaning, Reconstruction and the Experience of Loss*, American Psychological Association, Washington DC.

Oodgeroo of the Noonuccal (Kath Walker), 1964, *We are Going*, Jacaranda Press, Queensland.

Perry B.D. & Hambrick E., 2008, 'The Neurosequential Model of Therapeutics', *Reclaiming Children and Youth*, 17(3), pp38–43.

Plumber D., 2005, *Helping Adolescents and Adults to Build Self-Esteem*, Jessica Kingsley, London.

Roffey S., 2006, *Circle Time for Emotional Literacy*, Sage, London.

Roger J.E. (ed.), 2007, *The Art of Grief*, Routledge Taylor & Francis, New York.

Rubin G., 2005, 'Cyber Bullying', *Times Educational Supplement* 4617, pp11–14.

Saner E., 2009, 'The Comfort of Memorial Websites', *The Guardian*, 7 October 2009, p.10.

Schuurman D., 2003, *Never the Same*, St Martin's Press, New York.

Shipman C. et al., 2001, 'Responding to the Needs of Schools in Supporting Bereaved Children', *Bereavement Care* 20(3), pp6–7.

Silverman P.R. & Worden J.W., 1992, 'Children's Reactions in the Early Months After the Death of a Parent', *American Journal of Orthopsychiatry* 162(1), pp93–104.

Stokes J., 2004, *Then, Now and Always*, Winston's Wish, Cheltenham.

Stroebe M.S. & Schut H., 1999, 'The Dual Process Model of Coping with Bereavement: Rationale and Description', *Death Studies* 23, pp197–224.

Sunderland M., 2007, *What Every Parent Needs to Know*, Dorling Kindersley, London.

Sunderland M. (ed.), 2012, *Helping Teenagers with Anger & Low Self-Esteem*, Hinton House Publishers, Buckingham.

Thomas D., 1959, *Collected Poems*, Dent, London.

Williams A.L. & Merten M.J., 2009, 'Adolescents' Online Social Networking Following the Death of a Peer', *Journal of Adolescent Research* 24, pp67–90.

Worden W.J., 1996, *Children and Grief*, The Guildford Press, New York.

Also available from Hinton House

Supporting Fostered & Adopted Children through Grief & Loss
Practical Ideas & Creative Approaches

Lorna Miles & Anna Jacobs

All ages

Creative ideas and guidance for carers, social care staff and school professionals.

A child from the care system experiences multiple losses: family, home, friends, familiar environments and sometimes also bereavement. They can be confused about what is happening and what the future holds.

This book covers theory, understanding of the developmental and traumatic influences which have shaped children's behaviour and will provide hope to carers and others who offer this vital care.

Containing a wealth of ideas and creative approaches to encourage conversation and interaction, this resource aims to help children and those supporting them with emotions, relationships and behaviours using a range of mediums such as art, creative writing, storytelling and film.

192pp A4 paperback • 978-1906531-62-1 • **£29.99**

Supporting Children through Grief & Loss

Anna Jacobs

Ages 6-12

A wealth of advice and helpful suggestions for those helping children through bereavement and loss.

Children who experience loss through death or separation need support and understanding, both at home and at school.

We often struggle to know what to say and how to provide this support. Staff in schools need to understand what to say and what to do, what might help and even what might not, and how to work with families.

This book gives an overview of different behaviours you may encounter in school and how to respond, as well as discussing questions children may ask and how to answer them.

Children's understanding of death varies according to stage of development and the author provides guidance on age-appropriate, honest responses along with a toolkit of creative and arts activities to help children examine and understand their emotions, physical feelings and memories.

192pp A4 paperback • 978-1906531-53-9 • **£24.99**

Lucy's Story
A child's story grief and loss

Anna Jacobs

Ages 6-11

Once there was a happy child who had no cares and worries. She had a lovely mum, a wonderful dad, and a baby brother. But then it all went horribly wrong...

This illustrated therapeutic story is written from the point of view of a young girl whose father has died. It explores how she feels and reacts to the loss both within her family and at school, and shows how an isolated child such as Lucy can be given help and understanding.

Offers an explanation of the concepts of death and loss, and shows how children experience loss.

Can be used by schools, counsellors and families to support children who are experiencing loss, as well as to safely introduce concepts of bereavement within the classroom. Each chapter contains notes related to the issues of bereavement and loss with children of primary age.

36pp illustrated paperback • 978-1906531-60-7 • **£12.99**

Rory's Story
An Adolescent Story of Grief and Loss

Anna Jacobs

Ages 13+

'Rory picked himself up and looked down: his hands were full of gravel and blood... things were different now and he didn't know what to do about it...'

Rory is an adolescent boy who is struggling with the loss of his mother. Confused and bullied at school, he attempts to run away and finally returns to face his feelings.

This therapeutic story:

- Is a gritty, readable story that teenagers will relate to.
- Explores the teenage experience of loss and bereavement.
- Can be used to support young people who have experienced loss.
- Will help teenagers understand the needs of their peers when loss occurs.
- Has notes for discussion on the themes of each chapter.

This useful tool which will help teachers, therapists and carers to support and understand the needs of adolescents facing loss.

48pp A5 paperback • 978-1906531-42-3 • **£12.99**

Changes
A story to help young children when loss or change occurs

Anna Jacobs

Ages 3-7

This moving, simple book introduces the concepts of loss and change to very young children. It uses the power of nature to explain what loss may feel like, and uses simple, clear language which will aid understanding and discussion of feelings.

It is beautifully illustrated throughout and aims to build resilience in very young children by offering them hope, as well as suggesting ways to help difficult feelings. Because it is non-specific, it can be used with many different forms of loss, such as divorce and separation, bereavement and even moving house.

24pp Illustrated paperback • 978-1906531-41-6 • **£9.99**

www.hintonpublishers.com   e: sales@hintonpublishers.com

HINTONHOUSE